PENGUIN PLAYS

THREE TRAGEDIES

FEDERICO GARCÍA LORCA

FEDERICO GARCÍA LORCA

Three Tragedies

BLOOD WEDDING

YERMA

THE HOUSE OF BERNARDA ALBA

Translated by
James Graham-Luján and Richard L. O'Connell
Introduction by
Francisco García Lorca

PENGUIN BOOKS
IN ASSOCIATION WITH SECKER AND WARBURG

Penguin Books Ltd, Harmondsworth, Middlesex, England
Penguin Books Australia Ltd, Ringwood, Victoria, Australia

—

Bodas de Sangre first published 1933
This translation first published 1945 in America
Yerma first published 1935
This translation first published 1946 in America
La Casa de Bernarda Alba first published 1940
This translation first published 1941 in America
The three translations first published in England by Secker & Warburg 1959
Published in Penguin Books 1961
Reprinted 1967, 1969

—

Yerma first appeared in *From Lorca's Theatre, Five Plays of Federico García Lorca* (Scribners, 1941). It is reprinted by permission of Charles Scribner's Sons. The translation printed here has been completely revised.

Made and printed in Great Britain by
Western Printing Services Ltd, Bristol

CONTENTS

INTRODUCTION

I DO not know to what extent I should have accepted the writing of an introduction to these three plays of my brother. Having accepted the charge, I carry it out, but only after having overcome an inner resistance. Because I owed him so much both in life and after his death, it seems to me that with the writing of this I contribute, even in small measure, toward the payment of a debt of fraternal love. Yet, perhaps that debt should be left undisturbed.

For me, Federico's theatre begins with my first childhood memories. The first toy that Federico bought with his own money, by breaking open his savings bank, was a miniature theatre. He bought it in Granada, in a toy store called 'The North Star', which was on the Street of the Catholic Kings. No plays came with this little theatre, so they had to be made up. This must have been his first attempt at drama. There was also the real theatre, to which our parents often took us, awakening in us an affection for it from an early age. I remember that once in Málaga, during someone's relaxed watchfulness, we ran off to go to the theatre. They were giving a racy operetta, whose raciness we did not savour. It must have been an object of curiosity, to an audience of men, to see two boys, very grave and well-mannered, in a box by themselves.

But Federico was attracted by games of a theatrical nature even more than by the real theatre. He liked to play at theatre and at marionettes, to dress up the maids and make them go out into the street – grotesquely dressed sometimes, or dressed as ladies – wearing my mother's or my Aunt Isabel's street clothes. Priceless at these games was Dolores, my nurse, who became the model for the servants in *Blood Wedding* and in *Doña Rosita, the Spinster*. From her we heard our first folk-tales – those of the unforgettable 'Pot-thumper' – at the fireside while our parents passed an evening at the theatre. I can never forget one of our servants dressed as a Moor, in towel and curtains, plastered with rice powder, gravely reciting and half inventing 'The Alcázar of Pearls'. In her wonderful simplicity the poor woman did not realize how comic her performance was, but we, with the cruelty the young sometimes have, appreciated it fully. Make-believe, disguises, and masks charmed Federico the boy. They were like an unbreakable spell, for even then he had begun to transform the world of fiction into a living reality and to identify all of reality with a fantastic dream. Later he was to see life as a

9

sort of dramatic game, a 'great world stage'[1] that, though it did not lack a distant religious background, included a vaster world of mysteries and passions.

It is rarely that this dualism of art and life has been integrated in a fashion so simple, so spontaneous, and at the same time so profound.

I believe that this is exactly the opposite of certain 'modern' tendencies conducive to the living of a literary life. Valle-Inclán could serve as the supreme example of this tendency, for in time he became his own best literary creation. This is another manner of identifying life with art. The basic difference is that while for Valle-Inclán literary criteria predominated, for Federico the most important thing was life, with all its drama and confusion. Valle-Inclán's life was a consequence of his art; in Federico, art was a consequence of his life. This holds in so far as such generalizations are possible; in the strange alchemy of these transmutations it is not easy to say which is the predominant element. In general terms the statement seems to me a just one.

The final value of Federico's theatre, and the one which most characterizes it, is this fundamental attitude of an author who likes to live; that is to say, to suffer and enjoy life's course as an inevitable universal drama. It seems as though in Federico, both in his life and in his writing, the man was not alive except in his moments of laughter and tears, in his extreme moments of joy and sorrow. Other times are entr'actes. I remember that in our childhood we frequently played one of his favourite games. Before an altar made with an image of the Holy Virgin, loaded down with roses and celandines from the garden, he would play priest, costumed in the best he could find. My sisters, I, a few other children, and the servants would attend. The almost express and almost tacitly accepted condition was that we had to weep at the time of the sermon. Half in jest, we would weep. Dolores, Federico's ideal audience, would really weep.

Laughter and tears, tears above all, run through all his poetry. Federico is fundamentally an elegiac poet. And laughter and tears are the two poles of his theatre. This explains why all his work courses between tragedy and farce. His literary creatures, always poetic embodiments, are conceived either in a tragic sense or with the wry grimace of guignol characters. Poetry, laughter, and tears are the ingredients of his dramatic invention.

Into some of his plays people have tried to read 'concessions' to the audience. The fact is that he played for the laughter and tears of the audience which, in a way, never ceased being the Dolores of his childhood games. But communion or communication with people he felt as

1. The title of a Calderón play. *Translators' note.*

a true artist feels: primordially, with a noble sentiment. I do not deny that all sentiment is complex and that success might tempt him, but never to the point of making facile concessions opposed to this art's dignity. At heart I am convinced that he addressed himself to simple persons, or to what there can be of simplicity in persons who are not simple. Nothing could be further from him than to wish to touch what is called the 'chord of reason'. The audience he was thinking about can best be imagined by reading *The Shoemaker's Prodigious Wife*. Naturally, though, his theatre has many facets and it is not contradictory, but complementary, that he should write another type of play incomprehensible to a plain audience. *If Five Years Pass* is a much freer theatre exercise – one in which the spectator feels himself drawn by its mystery, its surprise, and by its values of pure plastic drama. Federico also came to feel the audience as a blind and threatening multitude, full of turbid passions. Against this multitude he wrote *The Audience*, an almost unplayable piece because of its scenic investiture, and one which I would choose as the most impetuous and dramatic exercise the surrealist theatre has produced. *If Five Years Pass* is to *The Audience* what *The Shoemaker's Prodigious Wife* is to *Yerma*.

But in either case – audience of plain folk or thousand-headed monster, family audience of his childhood sermons or sordid protagonist of blind passions – the theatre never ceased to be a passionate game to him, a transcript of life in which he played the role of 'author'. For in the same way that he appears in person in his poetry – 'How strange that my name should be Federico,' 'Ay, Federico García, call the Civil Guard!' – he appears in his plays. In some of them the author himself takes a part, and it is not by chance that in his last play, *The Dreams of My Cousin Aurelia*, of which he was able to write only the first act, the leading character is Federico himself as a child. He played as author, director, and character, and in this same game he made the audience the principal character of the play. And in all of this may be marked the desire, more or less conscious, of interchanging the planes of art and reality and of welding them, as they were welded by his life's marvellous impetus.

For his was an authentic living, if such there ever was. He was completely dedicated to his calling; not to his literary calling, but to his calling of living. Those who knew him will not forget his gift – I was about to say his unmatched gift – of enlivening things by his presence, of making them more intense. With him, everything was intensified to a degree. I remember that Jorge Guillén, great poet and Federico's great friend, would say: 'Federico's here. Now we'll go on a poetry bender.' Within his life's intensity was interwoven his art, an art which sprang in crystallized form almost without a break. In just one minute a poem could take form. The persons about him might any day become characters in his plays, as he himself might. A phrase spoken by him or by another would some day be printed in one of his books. So his work grew apace, in rhythm with his life and in as natural a fashion. This evolution of his work, growing with the spontaneity, the consequence, and the unity of a tree, has not been studied. Each phase is contained in the foregoing one; in his first book of poems all his later works are announced – including some which, as Don Federico de Onís says, did not reach fulfilment.

This interweaving of his life and work, this erasing of the limits between life and fiction, between man and poet, is equally real in the theatre: equally real between the playwright and his characters, we could say. How many times, as a game, he would pass whole hours talking like a maid in a rich house, like a little old convent lady, like a villager from Alpujarra. The exactness of the language, the intonation, and characterization were prodigious. How many characters created thus in a moment! It was not simple imitation but an untiring creation, conceived naturally, in its reality.

But the real person, the one created in a conversation, and the theatrical one were all integral parts of that world of Federico's: real and fantastic in one, full of live beings, and fictional entities. Many times he himself, as when he was the 'author' in his plays, was a dramatic personage in his own life. A very flesh-and-blood being, but nevertheless a mythical and elusive one. How many times, on the great stage of the world, his life was a performance. But how far this was from a histrionic and false attitude. For this was not the mere playing of the role of someone else, nor the affecting of facets not possessed; it included, sometimes, the exorcizing of the shadow which lay behind his gaze even during the contagious moments of his laughter. That is why I would say that, just as someone called him 'poet by the grace of God', he was a dramatist by the same grace.

It is not true that he turned to the theatre because he at length found lyrical mediums of expression inadequate, thus making the theatre a mere phase of his poetic evolution. Artistically, this is not true. Even had he not 'written for' the theatre until his poetic evolution was well advanced, the statement would still be artistically false. More than that, the facts attest the contrary. His first theatre piece, *The Butterfly's Evil Spell*,[1] was written at the same time as his first published poems. What

1. The title suggested by the impresario and dramatist Gregorio Martínez Sierra. Federico had named this play *The Least of Comedies*, a title which was rejected for reasons having to do with the advertising. The text of this play,

is more, the very first poems he wrote, even prior to the *Book of Poems*, coincided chronologically with a play that was left half-finished. It was an ingenious play, romantic, with an historical setting, abounding in sonorous tirades, out of which I still remember a stray verse or other – a very bad play and one which to me, then, seemed a great one.

All of this material from adolescence, abundant though it was, has been lost. I now fear that in this loss the poet's hand may have had a part.

If this first play to which I refer deserved to be lost, not so with all the poems. Many were not inferior to those included in his first book. There was in particular the one he called *Book of Suites*, of which I remember as one of the best the 'Suite of the Clocks' – their muffled echoes reach as far as *If Five Years Pass*. If my memory does not betray me, fragments out of this suite and out of others passed into later poems.

We may say, then, that his theatre is simultaneous with his poetry. The need for dramatic expression was as pressing in him as the need for lyric expression. Not to accept his dramatic forms as a basic need of his poetic expression would be as much as to say that after his success in the theatre he *might* have abandoned lyric poetry. We know that after *The House of Bernarda Alba* he wrote a book of sonnets for the purpose of acquiring discipline after the free forms of his last book of poems. These sonnets are today lost. The original manuscript was in the hands of a friend who died fighting at the front during the Civil War.

It has been said that Federico, better than other poets of his generation, represents the Spanish in poetry. Perhaps this national character is the clearer defined because of his dramatic roots, his vocation of identifying himself with the impulses of his country's people. Even his little songs many times take on, in mysterious and unanalysable ways, the profound voices of the earth. His poetry may not be separated from his drama. And both are sustained by a certain breath which is part of the epic, of the nationally representative. In this sense, the family of Camborios, Yerma, or the horseman out of 'Córdoba, distant and lonely', all have the same character of tragic *fatum*, of being 'marked', to say it in a Spanish way. The same way in which the poet was marked, and counter-proved with his life his work's true authenticity.

These popular essences, which give fragrance to his lyric poetry with an unmistakable stamp, are perhaps what will in a final sense also make his theatre endure. Let me explain that I take the word *popular* in a much wider sense than that which means purely *folklore*. I have already referred to an epic tendency, without which his *Gypsy Balladeer*, for example, missing the last few pages, has recently been found and was published by Secker and Warburg in *Five Plays*, 1965.

13

could not be understood, for it has in it much less of the popular, in the restrictive sense of folklore, than people often imagine.

What I wish to indicate by this, rather, is that his theatre – and this is his strength – springs from the same fountains as his lyric poetry, and that both are vessel of that anonymous and collective voice which is his country's – one which is in its essence a permanent voice even though it may change in tone with the times. For he, modern in rhythm with his contemporaries and attuned to the period's manner, to which he is in great part indebted, owns a traditional volume which is alive and, for its better part, not studied, which singles him out and distinguishes him from the others. But at bottom his manner of grasping his country's artistic and permanent substance did not greatly differ from the way in which he assimilated and lived the currents and artistic problems of his time. These currents were more temporal, also of more extensive scope. He was not the *homme de lettres*; even though his contacts with outside literatures might at first surprise one by their vastness, he was host to these by a sort of contamination, an inevitable absorption of poetic seed, more than through systematic study or deliberate purpose. I could tell, having in some cases been the conveying vessel, what scant, circumstantial knowledge he had of various foreign poets who are the bases of contemporary poetic movements.

His accent is modern because he was a modern man. That period of his verse called surrealist, poetry of subconscious or semiconscious associations, has been considered by some as an excursion to the very margins of his real path and by others as a tribute to a compelling necessity. Both statements are unfounded. Aside from the fact that I do not believe Federico was a surrealist *stricto sensu*, his *Poet in New York*, the book that best represents this period of his development, is nothing but the crystallizing of a phase already contained, as with the rest of his books, in his previous poetry and drama. The rightness of this type of poetry to the spiritual moment in which it was produced frees it from any nature of concession and marks it with that seal of authenticity that characterizes the work of a poet who makes his life poetic substance. Already, in *Poet in New York* itself, may be seen an opening toward a port of greater rest. The last poems announce the *Divan of the Tamarit*, a book whose poems were woven with the most subtle threads of his lyric gift, among the shadows and murmurings of the water in our Granada garden.

The Audience, the play that corresponds in his theatre to *Poet in New York* in his poems, was already announced in *If Five Years Pass*. This in its turn is the crystallization of a tendency always implicit in his theatre – that of handling dramatic values, whenever possible, with the freedom of purely poetic ones. Any interpretation of his theatre made from a viewpoint other than a poetic one will lead to wrong conclusions.

From *The Least of Comedies* to *The Dreams of My Cousin Aurelia* there is a clear, final aspiration, one in which various paths are tried in search for the point of fusion between poetry and drama. The most disparate works are joined by this unity of purpose. Precisely one of the characteristics which gives value to my brother's work – and no one will think it strange that I should point it out – is its diversity, richer perhaps than in other poets of his time, and its essential unity. This is no longer a unity between the various parts of his poetry and drama, but between the poetry and drama themselves, for to study them as separate entities would be useless. It is a unity which is finally an identification with the poet's living being.

I am surprised how in his last works – works which have undergone such a complex development – there appear, sublimated and transformed, themes which take my memory back to the poetry of his adolescence.

The close correspondence between his theatre and poetry I regard from a strictly technical point of view also. At times there has been an effort to regard his dramatic technique as having fallen short and to say that he did not master the theatre's resources until *Blood Wedding*. I believe that there is a certain confusion in this due, in part at least, to considering Federico as a lyric poet who *turned* to the theatre and had to fit himself into a calling not his own. It would be useful to return to his poetry the better to clear this point.

Probably all the poets of his time surpassed Federico in the perfection of their initial poetic forms. Beside the first books of the others – almost perfect books in the majority – the *Book of Poems* is an adolescent's book, as he himself says in the prologue, asking forgiveness for its imperfection. In spite of this, or perhaps because of it, his is the one among first books which contains the greatest poetic possibilities – or, to avoid a qualitative expression, the one with the most diverse possibilities. A book which has the unique value among those of his generation, a negative value if you wish, of being just that: an adolescent's book.

In his second book, *Songs*, the poet reduced himself to his medium, lessened his ambitions, rid himself of some delusions, and produced, simply, an almost perfect book. Some of this book's songs have not been surpassed in simplicity, depth, and lyricism. Very well then, in the theatre, since this genre has a greater, I would not say, difficulty, but rather, a more complicated technique, exactly the same thing happened to him. Between *Mariana Pineda* and *Perlimplín* technically, as long a road has been run as that which lay between his first books of poems.

Though I am sometimes beset by a prejudice against speaking in exalted terms, I must say, because it is true, that *Perlimplín* and *The Shoemaker's Prodigious Wife* are plays finished with a perfect fitting of the medium to the artistic purpose. Plays completely well carried off, that will endure as jewels of the minor forms of the Spanish theatre.

These works already envisage another of Federico's aspects, one not yet touched upon: that of his prose. It is often forgotten, before poetry's glinting name, that my brother wrote more prose than verse. A dialogued and poetic prose in its greater part, surely, but one that adds yet another facet to his changing and whole personality.

Once his technical progress in the theatre has been affirmed (a progress which, as with all true artists, is but the discovery of the proper mediums of expression) I believe that in a discussion of his command of theatrical values what is alluded to, and objected to, is his conception of drama itself.

I do not know whether it would be presumptuous of me to refer to a question of literary form here. Of late, however, there has been a tendency not only of representing poetry and the theatre as two worlds apart but of considering poet and dramatist as two irreconcilable beings. We have witnessed a scrupulous separation of forms, and within each form we have seen its 'purification'. That is, pure poetry, pure painting, pure music, etc. And lyric poetry, within this tendency, has come to be no longer poetry by excellence but by exclusion – and that with only certain modes of lyric expression allowable within it. That a poet should write for the theatre was frowned upon. I remember perfectly when my brother put on his *Mariana Pineda* – by now the presentation of his first play had been forgotten – this was disdainfully commented upon in the most refined literary circles. In this same fashion the term 'poetic drama' has been used to designate a sort of hybrid genus; there has been implicit in the expression a shade of condescension toward a poet's dramatic fickleness. For sometimes those who were not quite poets, but who could not yet write 'real' drama, would turn to this genre.

I for my part confess that I do not know of any great drama that is not poetic drama. As a consequence of such an adamant attitude – for the greater part forgotten now – criticism of a play would have had to consist of separating the poetic from the dramatic, even though both these values might be impossible to isolate.

In the Spanish tongue at least, practice has more or less coincided with theory during the contemporary period. Poets, in their majority, have not heard the call of the theatre. They have been purely lyric poets.

Federico has in reality been the poet who most signally opened the theatre's doors to poets. Or, to say it in another fashion, the one who turned the current of poetry into the Spanish-speaking theatre.

Naturally, what has gone before does not imply a confusion between lyric poetry and drama, nor a refusal to recognize that the theatre has its own mediums of expression. It is simply an affirmation of the legality of the poetic conception of drama and a statement that this in its turn has its own mediums of scenic expression to which the criteria of a realistic theatre, to call it so, cannot be applied.

I say this because, parallel to the exclusion of poetry from the theatre, drama as a class has seemed to become, aesthetically, a foster child of the nineteenth century's realistic novel. I do not believe it has been entirely by chance that in Spain the theatre's representative *par excellence* within this generation should be Benavente. And this in spite of the efforts of the so-named 'Generation of '98' to impart poetry to all genera. Unamuno even went to the extreme of saying from his point of view: 'Novel, that is to say, poem.' Benavente is a writer of great talent, but one who creates an unpoetic theatre, a theatre of manners, without national character and without great themes.

A poetic conception of the theatre does not imply, as I said before, ignorance of the mediums of expression proper to the theatre. A forgetting of this basic truth could detract from dramatic values and sidetrack them into lyric channels weakening to a play's structure. I have known few people as conscious of this theatrical truth as Federico himself. Few authors have learned as much from a disappointing experience as he. The whole development of his drama consists in a pruning of lyric branches till he arrives at *The House of Bernarda Alba*, where this conscious purpose culminates. His tendency to crystallize his drama, to reduce it to values of strict dramatic poetry can easily be proved by comparing the three plays which appear in this book. The gradation is unmistakably evident.

If he sometimes seems to forget this preoccupation, as happens in *Doña Rosita*, it is only an apparent forgetting. I can only pick out one lyric passage, that of the ballad of the three Manolas, as in a certain fashion independent from the play. All the other lyric passages have been made part of the drama's essence. The ballad to which I refer, used to underline the play's Granadine atmosphere, is but the commentary of a popular song, a *granadina*.

> Granada, Street of Elvira,
> the home of the Manolas,
> they who go to the Alhambra,
> the three and the four alone.

It amused Federico to make these anonymous beings out of a song characters in his play, along with many others in the same play who are taken from real life. The exception, perhaps, is the heroine, who constitutes a symbol of the Granadine. I do not know up to what conscious point this is true, but this Granadine feeling was an emotion which always compelled him and which explains certain forms, certain aspects of his poetry and drama. The game to which I have alluded, that of relating real persons to literary and invented ones, was very much the poet's, for he never forgot his childhood games; they are always present in his plays.

None of the other lyric passages may be separated from the play, for they obey one of its essential purposes: a fusion of laughter and tears with poetic intention. I have not deduced this purpose. The author told me of it while he was writing the play. I remember his words: 'If in certain scenes the audience doesn't know what to do, whether to laugh or to cry, that will be a success for me.' Of all the poet's plays this is the most Granadine – full of that unstruggling frustration which is at the basis of everything Granadine.

The hidden personage in the play is Granada. And in all his work there are hidden players, masked beings, poetic symbols, butterflies, steeds, dead children: blind forces who step out on the stage or who merely haunt it – and who mysteriously embody the character, the artistic profile of a race, its fate, its life, and dreams, its failure and death.

This intervention of hidden players became one of his technical resources. It is evident in *The House of Bernarda Alba*, for perhaps the most prominent character in this play never appears on the stage at all. Quietly, this device is in almost all his plays. That is why the same standards of criticism cannot be applied to this type of theatre as to a theatre on a basis that is not poetic. For in drama such as Federico's the characters (the leading characters much more than the minor ones) are rather in the nature of symbols than of individual beings. And this, in short, is what the great Spanish theatre has been able to do better than any other great theatre. Neither Don Juan, nor Fuente Ovejuna, nor the Mayor of Zalamea, nor Sigismund embody individual beings; neither may they be measured by a 'psychological' criterion. Nevertheless, there are no literary characters who better identify themselves with their audiences. There is no theatre which embodies more profoundly than the Spanish theatre the character, the hopes, the beliefs, and the dreams of the people of its country.

With his drama, Federico was the playwright who most resolutely in modern times turned toward real Spanish tradition – a tradition ignored in a surprising manner by Benavente himself.

I believe, as another example, that the same thing happened with his drama as with the modern or popular character of his poetry. Far from arising out of a deliberate or thoughtful purpose, this nature of his poetry was due to a coincidence of temperament or character.

This recapturing of tradition in order to express it in modern idiom is most evident in his verse. The *Gypsy Balladeer* is but the renewal of the most characteristic genre of Spanish traditional poetry, the ballad. What the great poets achieved with the ballad during the classical period, followed by the Duke of Rivas y Zorilla among the Romantics, that is Federico's achievement among the moderns.

And without my wishing to force an identification or a likeness of values between his poetry and his drama, I still believe that he brought about something analogous in the theatre. Aside from any coincidence already cited in speaking about the poetic idea of drama and of the conception of characters, in the history of the modern Spanish theatre Federico is the first to look toward our classic theatre in order to restore some of its essential qualities. Among these qualities is that of considering the theatre as a complete spectacle. Lyric passages that from today's preconceived notions about the theatre might be considered added or accessory are the ones which most strictly adhere to classic Spanish tradition. Our ancient theatre is a holiday – a great holiday for the spirit, for the eyes, and for the ears. No modern playwright has made the musical and the plastic share in the theatre to the extent that Federico did. And this was not done in an accessory or contrived fashion but rather by using these elements as part of the dramatic essence: integrated within the play's unity. Mr Edwin Honig, in his fine book,[1] has noted the melodic development, following a musician's criterion, of *If Five Years Pass* and of *Perlimplín*. In greater or lesser measure this criterion may be applied to the whole body of his work. We are not concerned, then, with the occasional presence of songs or dances, but with the participation of musical essences within the very conception of a play. Federico even rearranged some of his plays, accentuating the tendency referred to, until they became musical comedies or ballets.

That is why, such being his conception of theatre, in evaluating it one may speak about the degree to which he carried out his intention of filling the stage with poetry, of integrating certain traditional aspects with modern forms, of replying with his drama's characters to the anonymous voices of his land, of bringing to the theatre the restlessness and artistic problems of his time. One might ask to what measure he was able to make use of the resources of the theatre proper in order to attain these objectives. What one cannot do is apply to a drama that is poetic

1. *García Lorca*, by Edwin Honig, New Directions, 1944.

in conception and symbolical in its essence the standards of criticism applicable to a realistic and psychological drama.

I sometimes ask myself if Federico himself did not over-exaggerate his tendency of purging lyric elements from his drama. In this regard, *Yerma*, out of the trilogy that makes up this book, is perhaps the play which reaches the greatest balance between poetic, plastic, and dramatic elements. Federico could not have renounced – it would have been impossible – a poetic conception of the theatre. But in a certain way he also dedicated himself to search in his own fashion for a *pure* theatre. Within his dramatic conception (and only *Mariana Pineda* is not conceived dramatically) it became necessary to limit the sallies of the lyric poet in him. And, except for minor instances, in my judgement he succeeded in not allowing his plays to get beyond the control of a dramatic outline served by a notable economy of words.

The House of Bernarda Alba is but the culmination of this tendency, long before noted. I remember that the success obtained by a scene we might call lyric in *Yerma*'s second act, that of the Laundresses, during the play's run in Madrid was always considered by Federico a success little to be desired.

In his last play all this is radically suppressed. Sobriety becomes the essential motive in the play's conception. And this sobriety is converted almost into a display of virtuosity. He played to the audience, as I said before, but on his own terms. Far from insisting on those effects the public asked for, in seeking his audience he avoided the resources proved by success, in order to find his own audience on a higher level: either in the austere dramatic scheme of *Bernarda Alba*, or in the handling of dramatic material with a poem's freedom. Though at heart he was concerned with marking a road to the audience, he would not allow that audience to lead him along the road to an easy triumph. He fought his own battle between artistic freedom and discipline with his conscience gravely concerned with the problem of the enduring quality of his work. This conflict between freedom and discipline on the one hand, between poetry and reality on the other – or between nature and art, to state it in traditional terms – he lived with such intensity that it would not be mere conjecture to say that it took on a dramatic aspect within the poet himself. The drama rising from the heart of the Shoemaker's wife, a struggle between fantasy and reality, in the soul of Don Perlimplín, in Belisa's flesh, or in Yerma's innermost being, is the aesthetic drama of the poet himself. It is the conflict which the Spanish soul felt like none other and which Federico, to the measure which the conflict permitted, resolved after the Spanish fashion: by setting his roots in reality the better to make it poetic.

The ideas of Granada and of amorous frustration, such as appear in the song of the Three Manolas – they who carried up to the Alhambra their unmarried girls' loneliness – probably gave birth, among other things, to *Doña Rosita*. Most times Federico needed the support of some sort of reality, even a poetic or a musical one, upon which to construct.

A searching analysis of the elements of direct reality which enter either into his poetry or his drama would surprise one. Anyone could identify many of these elements. Del Río,[1] in his profound study, has already done this in part. I could identify many events or allusions to events out of real life; others, only the poet could point out, but the greater part perhaps not even the poet himself could identify. I say this because sometimes he assimilated these elements out of reality until he made them his own flesh. I doubt that he could have recognized the precise origin of some of the analogies between animals and water, and blood and water that so abound in his poetry. One time Dolores was describing the birth of a spring and in her picturesque and vivid speech she said: '. . . and imagine, a bull of water rose up'. I remembered the impression this admirable phrase made on Federico, for it appears later, more or less transformed, but particularly in these lines from the *Balladeer*:

> The heavy water bullocks
> charge against the boys
> who bathe inside the moons
> of their curving horns.

In this regard I remember a curious incident. During an excursion to the Sierra Nevada, the mule driver who was leading sang to himself:

> So I took her to the river,
> thinking she was a maiden,
> but she had a husband.

Some time later, one day when we were speaking of the ballad of 'The Faithless Wife', I reminded Federico of the mule driver's song. To my enormous surprise, he had completely forgotten it. He thought the first three lines of the ballad were as much his as the rest of the poem. More than that, I thought I could tell that he did not like my insistence, for he continued to believe that I was mistaken.

The references that del Río makes to the factual bases of some of the poems out of *Poet in New York* show that Federico's essential attitude toward poetry and his poetic resources and technique are the same

1. *Federico García Lorca, 1899–1936*. Vida y Obra, Bibliografía, Antología, Obras Inéditas, Música Popular. Hispanic Institute in the U.S. Columbia University. New York, 1941.

throughout the rich diversity of his work. Inversely, it remains a strange thing that in spite of the theatre's social dimension and this genre's necessarily more realistic character, there should nevertheless be a lesser play of fantastic and 'created' elements in it than in his poetry proper. Here also one may see the poet's identity – and his diversity. For there are no two plays in which reality assumes a part in the same fashion and to the same proportion.

Doña Rosita, perhaps the most lyric in tone of all the plays, contains more elements of reality in it than all the plays which preceded it. Naturally, there are different planes of reality in this work, as in almost all of them. Here, there is a reality made poetic: the atmosphere of Granada. It is what one might call the play's spirit, and it would still be in it even without a single direct reference – just as it exists, in another way, in *Don Perlimplín*. In *Doña Rosita* the evocation of the atmosphere, and of the period, is created without sparing a single detail. Proper names of Granada families, real happenings, real persons, and literary ones, appear. Some of the incidents which would seem most improbable spring straight from reality. Many of the phrases of the Economics Instructor – 'I do not possess a sufficient volume of experience . . .' 'The earth is a mediocre planet . . .' and others – are out of the speech of persons known in the Spanish faculty. Never till then had the poet so resorted to actual happenings as in this play, the only one for which he 'did research'.

I remember seeing 1,900 almanacs and magazines on his work-table in our Granada garden. The ballad about the language of the flowers was made from a little book that contained, besides the language of the flowers, that of stamps, the fan, dreams, etc. The allusions to automobile races and such other details are taken from books. What is more, the description of the *mutabile* rose, which constitutes the play's essence, and the descriptions of the *hispid* and *inermis* roses are data out of an old botany book which the poet, Moreno Villa, showed Federico, and which finally crystallized the idea of *Doña Rosita*.

This play haunted the poet's imagination for many years and was the longest in maturing among all that he wrote. Its conception was such a task to him that I know that when he saw it finished it was a load off his shoulders. To understand this statement better, one must know how Federico 'worked'; abandoning projects, forgetting themes, and then letting them be reborn in his memory to the spark of some new reality. More than by thinking things out, by allowing things – to say it with an Unamunesque phrase – to think him out: until those two worlds met and welded – which was the time to write. And then, what ease, what simplicity, and, at bottom, what joy in the task of creating.

But he would not spare his errors or his weaknesses until he overcame them. I believe that with *Doña Rosita*, written with great care, he overcame the private failure of *Mariana Pineda*. One can almost imagine something like a rivalry with the city of Granada itself – a desire to possess it artistically and to express it. From Mariana Pineda's lyric Granada he moved to a more complex Granada which he loved and disdained, over which he laughed and wept. I do not want to speak of the outcome of this relationship, which seems an awful vengeance of the city against the soul that best expressed it.

Likewise, to me, *The Love of Don Perlimplín* is the victory over that other frustrated exercise of his, *The Butterfly's Evil Spell*, with which this play has a number of thematic relationships. This is the Butterfly which, freed now, still flutters among the plays in *The Shoemaker's Prodigious Wife*.

This innate tenacity of his character surprises me, as I consider it today. It is a tenacity unperceived by those who saw him pass through life, voluble, vagabond, a troubadour.

Into the three plays that make up this book, reality enters in diverse fashions. Reality and dramatic (that is to say, poetic) values are balanced in different ways.

It has already been told how *Blood Wedding* was inspired by a newspaper account of an incident almost identical with the plot of the play, which took place in Almería. However, many years passed before he decided to write the play; it had a gestation period almost as long as *Doña Rosita* did.

After grasping reality, it was as though he needed to draw away from it, to dream on it anew, then to incorporate the live persons into his own poetic mythology. It is perfectly apparent that the characters in *Blood Wedding* went through this evolutionary process.

I do not know how many times he told me about the play. Then he would forget it; later it would reappear, but transformed (he never wrote down a play's outline) until, fully conceived at last in his fantasy, he wrote it. If I remember correctly, *Blood Wedding* only took a week to write; but in maturing it took years.

Most times he did not himself know what was going to happen in a play – yet it would later surprise me how he would have foreseen, in a first act, what would have its justification in a third. The part he turned over to a process of unconscious cerebration was enormous. And it is not only for such works as *If Five Years Pass* that this statement holds true, but in great measure for all of them.

His procedure in writing for the theatre did not vary greatly from the one he adopted for poetry. What was perhaps a play's essential part he entrusted to instinct. If he had not been a born playwright he could never have brought a dramatic work to realization.

In *Blood Wedding* there is a palpable (and I do not know if I should add, but involuntary) intention of taking the play's atmosphere away from any nature of a newspaper story. From the field of the very human passions of concrete beings he removes to an unreal world, one in which the appearances of mysterious and fantastic players (as in the personification of the Moon and Death) are possible. Then he makes the flesh-and-blood characters rise to a plane less real, one which converts them into forces whose incentives are outside themselves. At the play's climax, one of the characters says this:

> For the fault is not mine;
> the fault is the earth's.

And a lesser one:

> Blood that sees the light
> is drunk up by the earth.

In this fusion with nature – for more than nature it is Earth herself they tread on – the characters have lost individuality. They have moved away from the newspaper account from which they came but they have gained in human and poetic significance. They have been converted into anonymous beings who possess a country's generic character, who are opposed by a tragic personage, their fate, and who are led by this fate among songs and premonitions toward death. As the great poet, Pedro Salinas, says, '*Blood Wedding* gives body, dramatic realization, and the category of great art to a concept of human life borne along time's length in a people's innermost being and traditionally remembered and kept alive in it: the concept of human fatality.'[1]

Thus there is a greater abundance of poetic themes in this work; the turning to verse in climactic situations is frequent. Even more: the moments of the play's greatest dramatic intensity are in verse. But Federico never turns to this technical device without a careful preparation. The final episode of the next to last scene, an episode unequalled in dramatic sensuality, is preceded by a series of fantastic appearances which makes the use of verse and of the characters' poetic expressions seem natural. This to such a degree that the episode is imbued with a tone that surpasses in realism the scenes of greater realistic intention.

To some critics this is the play which best achieves an integration of

1. *Literatura española del siglo XX*, by Pedro Salinas. Editorial Seneca. México, 1941.

poetry and drama. It is the most spontaneous and simple because the poet does not struggle against his poetic instinct; he gives himself over to it, but without forgetfulness of his previous experiences.

In spite of this, Federico considered that his theatre would benefit by a more austere technique, progressing toward drama by the roads furthest removed from lyric forms. It is curious that in *Yerma*, while seeking a design simpler in elements and further purged of the ingredients of fantasy, instead of staying closer to reality he moved away from it. Of the trilogy contained in this book, *Yerma* is the play which has the smallest number of elements directly inspired by reality. Federico turned to a theme present in all his lyric and dramatic work – that of a frustrated instinct for motherhood; this theme he embodied in the character that is the most symbolic in all his theatre, perhaps the most dramatic and, I was about to say, the most poetic.

The drama centres about the violence with which the main character lives her personal conflict. It has been argued – a little childishly, to my notion – that Yerma's dramatic obsession is not entirely justified psychologically, since it could have a solution. And in effect, it could have one, and there would be no drama, by making Yerma cease to be Yerma – that is to say, by making her cease to feel her maternal instinct tragically. Or, with the easy solution (entirely problematical in another sense) of changing men. It would not be worth the effort to falsify Yerma's character by making her violate her sense of duty – another defining trait of her character – so that afterward she might continue being Yerma as before. This solution is proposed in the play and rejected.

In spite of the fact that in *Yerma* reality appears as the well of direct inspiration in lesser measure than in the other two plays, the secondary characters, to my judgement, have a greater individuality than those in *Blood Wedding*. In spite of Yerma's poetic atmosphere, in spite of the fact that in it poetic speech – which continues to have that characteristic poetic realism – is not abandoned but simply made purer, the characters no longer live submissive to forces extraneous and superior to themselves, but with themselves as centres. As a case in point, I cite that the Moon does not, as in *Blood Wedding*, prepare the blood's pathway. The Pagan Crone (in all his theatre, one of the characters most alive) chooses her own road as, fundamentally, Yerma herself does.

The drama is not determined by external accidents or, finally, by such chance as the meeting of two persons. In *Blood Wedding*, a knife can be drama's final reason. The poet is shaken that an insignificant hazard, an inert and tiny object, should be able to put an end to the blood's live torrent. But in *Yerma* the conflict is determined by a force that struggles against itself within the soul. A violent anxiety of fertility and sterility, or on another plane, of life and death – as in all of Federico's plays. Man's essential drama.

The instrument which brings death to that child who never existed except in the form of a desperate hope is Yerma herself. The solution, if the term may be so used, she gives out of her own flesh. It is the right thing for the play that Yerma should kill with her own hands and not with a knife, as in *Blood Wedding*; those hands held the power of death, embodied by now in the central character herself. In the final scene, prepared by a frenzied dance to life, what is mourned is nothing other than the symbolic death of Yerma, now without direction or justification. It is Yerma who dies, just as it was she who was in final agony before. In the play's dramatic conception everything is a reference to the single character. Unamuno's name in relation to *Yerma* has also already been recalled. At the play's dress rehearsal in Madrid Don Miguel was present. With great generosity, he said to the author: 'This is the play I wish I had written.'

A confluence of traditional Spanish theatre tendencies, plastic and musical, is brought about in this play. This is achieved in a purer classic conception, toward which the poet turned his eyes in search for simplicity and sobriety. It is already expressed in the very title, *Yerma* – 'Barren'. An invented name, symbolic, univocal, which answers the play's conception in a perfect fashion.

Apropos of this, let me be forgiven if I recall the sureness and exactness with which Federico named his plays. Common, everyday objects he liked to call by fantastic and capricious names – many times by invented ones; and he carried this game, like others, to his life's end. But poetic things he liked to call by their own names. He is perhaps the only poet of his generation who did not endow his books of poems with literary names. His first book is called, simply, *Book of Poems*. He called *Songs* a book of songs and *Gypsy Balladeer* a book of ballads. Other titles stand as examples of the tendency: *Poems of the Cante Jondo*, *Lament for Ignacio Sánchez Mejías*, *Poet in New York*.

The only exception, and this but a relative one, is the book written in homage to the Arabic Andalusian poets, the *Divan of the Tamarit*. Here the literary lies in the use of the word 'divan' to mean collection; it is otherwise justified, however, since Tamarit is the Arabic name for the district in which the Granadine garden where this book was written is situated.

The same thing could be said of his plays. Wherever a literary name is used, an ironic allusion that goes beyond the term's aptness is implied, as in the sub-title of *Doña Rosita, the Spinster*, which is, *The Language of the Flowers*. Take too *The Love of Don Perlimplín and Belisa in the Garden*

– a play which the poet has called an 'allelujah'.[1] Particularly meaning-ful is the title *If Five Years Pass* for, beyond its poetic implication, the phrase might be the exact wording in simple prose of what happens in the play. Everywhere in Federico we find a double affirmation of poetry and truth.

Of the titles which make up this trilogy we have already cited *Yerma*. *Blood Wedding* is the only one which makes no reference to a proper name: the most directly poetic of the three titles, and the least per-sonalized.

In *Blood Wedding* the theme – as the poet promises and fulfils – is more the noun, *wedding*, than the characters themselves. Thus in the cast appear the Mother, the Bridegroom, the Bride, etc. But there is only one character with a name of his own – Leonardo: the most realistic character in the play, and the most 'biographical'. Though he also is destroyed by his destiny, he, more than the others, moves toward events of his own will. It is not that his will is stronger than that of the Mother or the Bride, but that things happen to them, while basic-ally he, Leonardo, goes looking for them to happen. The most dramatic character is the Mother; to her the greatest number of things outside the radius of her will happen. She is the chosen character of the blind forces. That is why Leonardo, the most individualized character, is the one who least stands out, the one who is furthest from the conception expressed in the title, *Blood Wedding*. And this in spite of the fact that that blood is his.

Yerma is the transition point toward *The House of Bernarda Alba*. And in this latter, just the opposite of *Blood Wedding*, all the characters have names. The title, which alludes to a family atmosphere dominated by one figure, applies to the context with the same exactness and expresses the dramatic conception which guided the poet. Bernarda Alba is no longer only a given name, but a family name. Even the oppressive monotony of a dominant and tyrannical character is expressed in the magnificent alliteration of the *a*'s: *La Casa de Bernarda Alba*.

This play, as was previously indicated, boasts such economy of lyric elements as to make almost a display of virtuosity out of it. The poet intensified his own tendencies to such an extreme that he achieved a work that lies at the furthest point of his drama's roads. Even though his own express statement would not be needed for an interpretation such as this, he did tell me that with this play he closed the cycle, gathered in

1. *An Erotic Allelujah in Four Scenes. Aleluya* is the Spanish name given to a particular kind of decorated valentines, made of paper, and with flowery couplets printed on them, which are distributed on certain festive days. *Translators' note.*

this trilogy, of rural dramas – a cycle so alike in its character and themes, so diverse in conception and technical resources.

The House of Bernarda Alba, of these plays, is the one which has the most direct inspiration in reality. In this it is the exact opposite of *Blood Wedding*, in which everything is invented except the plot. In *Bernarda*, everything except the story is inspired by reality. The story was potentially possible in the given setting; the characters are modified, as is natural, to make the plot possible.

But not a single one of the characters, even those who do not take part but are merely alluded to, and not a single act of those who serve as background proceed directly from the poet's imagination. And in spite of this basic reality, I would say that this is his most artful play and the one which is most disciplined in technique. In a certain way, it is the most *artistic* in its strangeness. His tendency of making female characters the most important ones in his theatre is accentuated until he produces a drama of women only.

We have already pointed out other characteristics of this creation – a creation so singular in its development, combining through a rare mystery the greatest contention and the greatest violence. Here are a starkness and intensity such as by another road were achieved by Don Miguel de Unamuno, whose name we often come across in analysing Federico's work. Federico's theatre cannot be completely understood if we do not look to the work of the famous Rector of Salamanca and to Valle-Inclán's. Though Federico's theatre is never near to the modernist tone of the latter's work, it conserves its poetic conception, its tone of tragedy or farce. And it is near to Unamuno's passionate schematism – but with a touch of Andalusian grace, an avocation for the plastic and the musical, which the great Basque did not possess.

Bernarda as a drama is characterized not only by the part played by reality, but by the interpretation of this reality, since the real basis only provides the artistic matter. In the play I think we may perceive a certain type of realism – and this is an approach already anticipated in others of his plays – nearer to the interpretive forms which have been considered as typically representative of what is Spanish.

In no other work of the author's do we find with such power the affirmation of the character of the personages, the defence of their individuality. Others of his poetic creatures, since they are conceived on another plane, struggle against their destinies, but at bottom convinced that it is impossible to overcome the unappeasable forces which play with man's fate.

'You have to follow the blood's road . . .' 'When things reach their centres . . .' – there is no one who can stand against them. Certainly this conformity with destiny – to say it with a religious word, this resignation – is human and Spanish. But it also is, and more representatively so, in a certain way, the will's steadfastness before destiny and before death. In this sense, the psychological attitude of the characters has changed in *The House of Bernarda Alba*.

And the play's dramatic tension is born precisely out of the clash of these wills. Of the domineering will of the mother, upheld by the forces of tradition, of custom, of social values – and of the deaf and invincible wills of the daughters, dragged by their thirst for living and by impulses and instincts which clash with each other in their turn. And over all of them, a tragic sense of life against which nothing avails. That is why it is curious and why it underscores the attitude of the central character that, when she is faced with the death of the daughter who has hanged herself with the cord with which the mother symbolically would have bound all of them, Bernarda finishes the drama with a shout of triumph, an illusory triumph, like Doña Perfecta's.

Here it would be opportune to cite the different road down which the playwright turned to achieve an artistic interpretation of reality. Before, the poet's world abounded either in signs and objects which were already poetic in themselves or else in everyday objects which had been put through the tollhouse of his poetry. Now he put himself to the test not only of permitting ugly or vulgar realities to enter into his world, but of selecting them with this very criterion in mind. On the other hand, however, I believe I can perceive that his literary tone has not much changed. In the other works there is a point of poetic violence, reiterated evidence of life's dramatic poetry. Here there is rather the somewhat anguished reiteration of the dark shadows that fall across a daily life. One could say that it is not so much that his eyes have changed, but that they are looking on reality's other aspect – and that out of this he achieved a stylization as literary as that of his other works. Perhaps more. I dare to hazard that *The House of Bernarda Alba* could be a fecund way to deepen what has been called Spanish reality. It surprises me how the same poet who has struck the greatest note of tenderness in the Spanish theatre could strip himself of it to the point which he has been able to do in this play. Everything has been foreset to avoid the temptations of turning to lyricism or tenderness. Here is a dark, closed recess into which the atmosphere's flooding light, the flesh's dolorous passion, and the tragic fate of persons filter through the bars. It is a symbol of the poet's own aesthetic position. The world with all its harshness, against which Bernarda and her daughters vainly defend themselves, passes before their windows in visions full of fury or drunk with dirty eroticism. These are the visions which burned the poet's imagination as a child, and which he now recasts in a defined scheme, sure and palpitant with truth. Scenes of lights and violence, hard, Goyesque – somewhat, and infinitely Spanish. And there, among these woman-figures, contained, self-burning, dark-souled – the serving women, trailing a low and picaresque undertone. This outlook arrives at something like a new, different vision by the force of surpassing previous stages. But as it happens, his work's enormous coherence makes it apparent that this aspect of reality had already been announced and expressed in previous moments of his poetry and drama. As at other times, what he has done is to isolate and construct upon materials contained in his previous work.

The fact of his being gifted with that very Spanish acumen of discovering the negative side of things confirms – and constitutes one of the reasons for his power – his sensitivity to all aspects of poetry. He has the facings of the three traditional poetic fronts: epic, lyric, and dramatic. I do not here concern myself, as may be seen, with anything save a recapitulation of values – and for this purpose it is enough for me not to falsify them. It could be said that all the important poets of his time and his tongue surpassed him in something, but he surpassed them all in the poetic integration of his work – a complete work.

It is the privilege of the lyric poet to cultivate his own medium, to clarify and deepen it until it has become perfect and unimprovable. It is the privilege of men like my brother to be open to all the calls of poetry, to its innumerable voices, and to be able to follow it to all its redoubts. Consequently there are poets who, in different intensities, are always doing over the same things. Federico was always doing different things, following poetry along different paths – even at those times when he seemed to continue along one path, as may be seen in this trilogy.

And within his work's variety which, for the reasons before expressed, has to be very high, unity is assured because of the unflagging poetic ability of the man who interwove his life and death with his work, and who already during his life was, among those who knew him, something of a legendary poet.

Francisco García Lorca

BLOOD WEDDING

*Tragedy in Three Acts
and Seven Scenes*

NOTICE

This edition of *Blood Wedding* has been
printed with the proper authorization. It
was scrupulously revised in accordance with
the original manuscript of Federico García
Lorca which I have in my possession, and it
contains his very latest revisions.

MARGARITA XIRGU

Buenos Aires, July 1938

Characters

—

THE MOTHER
THE BRIDE
THE MOTHER-IN-LAW
LEONARDO'S WIFE
THE SERVANT WOMAN
THE NEIGHBOUR WOMAN
THREE YOUNG GIRLS
LEONARDO
THE BRIDEGROOM
THE BRIDE'S FATHER
THE MOON
DEATH (*as a Beggar Woman*)
THREE WOODCUTTERS
TWO YOUNG MEN
THREE GUESTS

ACT ONE

SCENE I

A room painted yellow.

BRIDEGROOM [*entering*]: Mother.

MOTHER: What?

BRIDEGROOM: I'm going.

MOTHER: Where?

BRIDEGROOM: To the vineyard.

[*He starts to go.*]

MOTHER: Wait.

BRIDEGROOM: You want something?

MOTHER: Your breakfast, son.

BRIDEGROOM: Forget it. I'll eat grapes. Give me the knife.

MOTHER: What for?

BRIDEGROOM [*laughing*]: To cut the grapes with.

MOTHER [*muttering as she looks for the knife*]: Knives, knives. Cursed be all knives, and the scoundrel who invented them.

BRIDEGROOM: Let's talk about something else.

MOTHER: And guns and pistols and the smallest little knife – and even hoes and pitchforks.

BRIDEGROOM: All right.

MOTHER: Everything that can slice a man's body. A handsome man, full of young life, who goes out to the vineyards or to his own olive groves – his own because he's inherited them . . .

BRIDEGROOM [*lowering his head*]: Be quiet.

MOTHER: . . . and then that man doesn't come back. Or if he does come back it's only for someone to cover him over with a palm leaf or a plate of rock salt so he won't bloat. I don't know how you dare carry a knife on your body – or how I let this serpent

[*She takes a knife from a kitchen chest.*]

stay in the chest.

BRIDEGROOM: Have you had your say?

MOTHER: If I lived to be a hundred I'd talk of nothing else. First your father; to me he smelled like a carnation and I had him for barely three years. Then your brother. Oh, is it right – how can it be – that a small thing like a knife or a pistol can finish off a man – a bull of a man? No, I'll never be quiet. The months pass and the hopelessness of it stings in my eyes and even to the roots of my hair.

BRIDEGROOM [*forcefully*]: Let's quit this talk!

MOTHER: No. No. Let's not quit this talk. Can anyone bring me your father back? Or your brother? Then there's the jail. What do they mean, jail? They eat there, smoke there, play music there! My dead men choking with weeds, silent, turning to dust. Two men like two beautiful flowers. The killers in jail, carefree, looking at the mountains.

BRIDEGROOM: Do you want me to go kill them?

MOTHER: No . . . If I talk about it it's because . . . Oh, how can I help talking about it, seeing you go out that door? It's . . . I don't like you to carry a knife. It's just that . . . that I wish you wouldn't go out to the fields.

BRIDEGROOM [*laughing*]: Oh, come now!

MOTHER: I'd like it if you were a woman. Then you wouldn't be going out to the arroyo now and we'd both of us embroider flounces and little woolly dogs.

BRIDEGROOM [*he puts his arm around his mother and laughs*]: Mother, what if I should take you with me to the vineyards?

MOTHER: What would an old lady do in the vineyards? Were you going to put me down under the young vines?

BRIDEGROOM [*lifting her in his arms*]: Old lady, old lady – you little old, little old lady!

MOTHER: Your father, he used to take me. That's the way with men of good stock; good blood. Your grandfather left a son on every corner. That's what I like. Men, men; wheat, wheat.

BRIDEGROOM: And I, Mother?

MOTHER: You, what?

BRIDEGROOM: Do I need to tell you again?

MOTHER [*seriously*]: Oh!

BRIDEGROOM: Do you think it's bad?

MOTHER: No.

BRIDEGROOM: Well, then?

MOTHER: I don't really know. Like this, suddenly, it always surprises me. I know the girl is good. Isn't she? Well behaved. Hard working. Kneads her bread, sews her skirts, but even so when I say her name I feel as though someone had hit me on the forehead with a rock.

BRIDEGROOM: Foolishness.

MOTHER: More than foolishness. I'll be left alone. Now only you are left me – I hate to see you go.

BRIDEGROOM: But you'll come with us.

MOTHER: No. I can't leave your father and brother here alone. I have to go to them every morning and if I go away it's possible one of the Félix family, one of the killers, might die – and they'd bury him next to ours. And that'll never happen! Oh, no! That'll never happen! Because I'd dig them out with my nails and, all by myself, crush them against the wall.

BRIDEGROOM [*sternly*]: There you go again.

MOTHER: Forgive me.

[*Pause.*]

How long have you known her?

BRIDEGROOM: Three years. I've been able to buy the vineyard.

MOTHER: Three years. She used to have another sweetheart, didn't she?

BRIDEGROOM: I don't know. I don't think so. Girls have to look at what they'll marry.

MOTHER: Yes. I looked at nobody. I looked at your father, and when they killed him I looked at the wall in front of me. One woman with one man, and that's all.

BRIDEGROOM: You know my girl's good.

MOTHER: I don't doubt it. All the same, I'm sorry not to have known what her mother was like.

BRIDEGROOM: What difference does it make now?

MOTHER [*looking at him*]: Son.

BRIDEGROOM: What is it?

MOTHER: That's true! You're right! When do you want me to ask for her?

BRIDEGROOM [*happily*]: Does Sunday seem all right to you?

MOTHER [*seriously*]: I'll take her the bronze earrings, they're very old – and you buy her . . .

BRIDEGROOM: You know more about that . . .

MOTHER: . . . you buy her some open-work stockings – and for you, two suits – three! I have no one but you now!

BRIDEGROOM: I'm going. Tomorrow I'll go see her.

MOTHER: Yes, yes – and see if you can make me happy with six grandchildren – or as many as you want, since your father didn't live to give them to me.

BRIDEGROOM: The first-born for you!

MOTHER: Yes, but have some girls. I want to embroider and make lace, and be at peace.

BRIDEGROOM: I'm sure you'll love my wife.

MOTHER: I'll love her.

[*She starts to kiss him but changes her mind.*]

Go on. You're too big now for kisses. Give them to your wife.

[*Pause. To herself*]

When she is your wife.

BRIDEGROOM: I'm going.

MOTHER: And that land around the little mill – work it over. You've not taken good care of it.

BRIDEGROOM: You're right. I will.

MOTHER: God keep you.

[*The* SON *goes out. The* MOTHER *remains seated – her back to the door. A* NEIGHBOUR WOMAN *with a kerchief on her head appears in the door.*]

Come in.

NEIGHBOUR: How are you?

MOTHER: Just as you see me.

NEIGHBOUR: I came down to the store and stopped in to see you. We live so far away!

MOTHER: It's twenty years since I've been up to the top of the street.

NEIGHBOUR: You're looking well.

MOTHER: You think so?

NEIGHBOUR: Things happen. Two days ago they brought in my neighbour's son with both arms sliced off by the machine.
[*She sits down.*]

MOTHER: Rafael?

NEIGHBOUR: Yes. And there you have him. Many times I've thought your son and mine are better off where they are – sleeping, resting – not running the risk of being left helpless.

MOTHER: Hush. That's all just something thought up – but no consolation.

NEIGHBOUR [*sighing*]: Ay!

MOTHER [*sighing*]: Ay!
[*Pause.*]

NEIGHBOUR [*sadly*]: Where's your son?

MOTHER: He went out.

NEIGHBOUR: He finally bought the vineyard!

MOTHER: He was lucky.

NEIGHBOUR: Now he'll get married.

MOTHER [*as though reminded of something, she draws her chair near the* NEIGHBOUR]: Listen.

NEIGHBOUR [*in a confidential manner*]: Yes. What is it?

MOTHER: You know my son's sweetheart?

NEIGHBOUR: A good girl!

MOTHER: Yes, but . . .

NEIGHBOUR: But who knows her really well? There's nobody. She lives out there alone with her father – so far away – fifteen miles from the nearest house. But she's a good girl. Used to being alone.

MOTHER: And her mother?

NEIGHBOUR: Her mother I *did* know. Beautiful. Her face glowed like a saint's – but *I* never liked her. She didn't love her husband.

MOTHER [*sternly*]: Well, what a lot of things certain people know!

37

NEIGHBOUR: I'm sorry. I didn't mean to offend – but it's true. Now, whether she was decent or not nobody said. That wasn't discussed. She was haughty.

MOTHER: There you go again!

NEIGHBOUR: You asked me.

MOTHER: I wish no one knew anything about them – either the live one or the dead one – that they were like two thistles no one even names but cuts off at the right moment.

NEIGHBOUR: You're right. Your son is worth a lot.

MOTHER: Yes – a lot. That's why I look after him. They told me the girl had a sweetheart some time ago.

NEIGHBOUR: She was about fifteen. He's been married two years now – to a cousin of hers, as a matter of fact. But nobody remembers about their engagement.

MOTHER: How do you remember it?

NEIGHBOUR: Oh, what questions you ask!

MOTHER: We like to know all about the things that hurt us. Who was the boy?

NEIGHBOUR: Leonardo.

MOTHER: What Leonardo?

NEIGHBOUR: Leonardo Félix.

MOTHER: Félix!

NEIGHBOUR: Yes, but – how is Leonardo to blame for anything? He was eight years old when those things happened.

MOTHER: That's true. But I hear that name – Félix – and it's all the same.

   [*Muttering*]

Félix, a slimy mouthful.

   [*She spits.*]

It makes me spit – spit so I won't kill!

NEIGHBOUR: Control yourself. What good will it do?

MOTHER: No good. But you see how it is.

NEIGHBOUR: Don't get in the way of your son's happiness. Don't say anything to him. You're old. So am I. It's time for you and me to keep quiet.

MOTHER: I'll say nothing to him.

NEIGHBOUR [*kissing her*]: Nothing.

MOTHER [*calmly*]: Such things . . . !

NEIGHBOUR: I'm going. My men will soon be coming in from the fields.

MOTHER: Have you ever known such a hot sun?

NEIGHBOUR: The children carrying water out to the reapers are black with it. Good-bye, woman.

MOTHER: Good-bye.

[*Exit* NEIGHBOUR.]

[THE MOTHER *starts toward the door at the left. Half-way there she stops and slowly crosses herself.*]

CURTAIN

ACT ONE

SCENE 2

A room painted rose with copperware and wreaths of common flowers. In the centre of the room is a table with a tablecloth. It is morning.

> [*Leonardo's* MOTHER-IN-LAW *sits in one corner holding a child in her arms and rocking it. His* WIFE *is in the other corner mending stockings.*]

MOTHER-IN-LAW:

> Lullaby, my baby
> once there was a big horse
> who didn't like water.
> The water was black there
> under the branches.
> When it reached the bridge
> it stopped and it sang.
> Who can say, my baby,
> what the stream holds
> with its long tail
> in its green parlour?

WIFE [*softly*]:

> Carnation, sleep and dream,
> the horse won't drink from the stream.

MOTHER-IN-LAW:

> My rose, asleep now lie,
> the horse is starting to cry.
> His poor hooves were bleeding,
> his long mane was frozen,
> and deep in his eyes
> stuck a silvery dagger.
> Down he went to the river,
> Oh, down he went down!

40

And his blood was running,
Oh, more than the water.

WIFE:

Carnation, sleep and dream,
the horse won't drink from the stream.

MOTHER-IN-LAW:

My rose, asleep now lie,
the horse is starting to cry.

WIFE:

He never did touch
the dank river shore
though his muzzle was warm
and with silvery flies.
So, to the hard mountains
he could only whinny
just when the dead stream
covered his throat.
Ay-y-y, for the big horse
who didn't like water!
Ay-y-y, for the snow-wound
big horse of the dawn!

MOTHER-IN-LAW:

Don't come in! Stop him
and close up the window
with branches of dreams
and a dream of branches.

WIFE:

My baby is sleeping.

MOTHER-IN-LAW:

My baby is quiet.

WIFE:

Look, horse, my baby
has him a pillow.

MOTHER-IN-LAW:

His cradle is metal.

WIFE:

His quilt a fine fabric.

MOTHER-IN-LAW:

Lullaby, my baby.

WIFE:

Ay-y-y, for the big horse
who didn't like water!

MOTHER-IN-LAW:

Don't come near, don't come in!
Go away to the mountains
and through the grey valleys,
that's where your mare is.

WIFE [looking at the baby]:

My baby is sleeping.

MOTHER-IN-LAW:

My baby is resting.

WIFE [softly]:

Carnation, sleep and dream,
The horse won't drink from the stream.

MOTHER-IN-LAW [getting up, very softly]:

My rose, asleep now lie
for the horse is starting to cry.

[She carries the child out. LEONARDO enters.]

LEONARDO: Where's the baby?

WIFE: He's sleeping.

LEONARDO: Yesterday he wasn't well. He cried during the
night.

WIFE: Today he's like a dahlia. And you? Were you at the black-
smith's?

LEONARDO: I've just come from there. Would you believe it? For
more than two months he's been putting new shoes on the horse
and they're always coming off. As far as I can see he pulls them off
on the stones.

WIFE: Couldn't it just be that you use him so much?

LEONARDO: No. I almost never use him.

WIFE: Yesterday the neighbours told me they'd seen you on the far side of the plains.

LEONARDO: Who said that?

WIFE: The women who gather capers. It certainly surprised me. Was it you?

LEONARDO: No. What would I be doing there, in that wasteland?

WIFE: That's what I said. But the horse was streaming sweat.

LEONARDO: Did you see him?

WIFE: No. Mother did.

LEONARDO: Is she with the baby?

WIFE: Yes. Do you want some lemonade?

LEONARDO: With good cold water.

WIFE: And then you didn't come to eat!

LEONARDO: I was with the wheat weighers. They always hold me up.

WIFE [*very tenderly, while she makes the lemonade*]: Did they pay you a good price?

LEONARDO: Fair.

WIFE: I need a new dress and the baby a bonnet with ribbons.

LEONARDO [*getting up*]: I'm going to take a look at him.

WIFE: Be careful. He's asleep.

MOTHER-IN-LAW [*coming in*]: Well! Who's been racing the horse that way? He's down there, worn out, his eyes popping from their sockets as though he'd come from the ends of the earth.

LEONARDO [*acidly*]: I have.

MOTHER-IN-LAW: Oh, excuse me! He's your horse.

WIFE [*timidly*]: He was at the wheat buyers.

MOTHER-IN-LAW: He can burst for all of me!

[*She sits down. Pause.*]

WIFE: Your drink. Is it cold?

LEONARDO: Yes.

WIFE: Did you hear they're going to ask for my cousin?

LEONARDO: When?

WIFE: Tomorrow. The wedding will be within a month. I hope they're going to invite us.

LEONARDO [*gravely*]: I don't know.

MOTHER-IN-LAW: His mother, I think, wasn't very happy about the match.

LEONARDO: Well, she may be right. She's a girl to be careful with.

WIFE: I don't like to have you thinking bad things about a good girl.

MOTHER-IN-LAW [*meaningfully*]: If he does, it's because he knows her. Didn't you know he courted her for three years?

LEONARDO: But I left her.

[*To his* WIFE]

Are you going to cry now? Quit that!

[*He brusquely pulls her hands away from her face.*]

Let's go see the baby.

[*They go in with their arms around each other. A* GIRL *appears. She is happy. She enters running.*]

GIRL: Señora.

MOTHER-IN-LAW: What is it?

GIRL: The groom came to the store and he's bought the best of everything they had.

MOTHER-IN-LAW: Was he alone?

GIRL: No. With his mother. Stern, tall.

[*She imitates her.*]

And such extravagance!

MOTHER-IN-LAW: They have money.

GIRL: And they bought some open-work stockings! Oh, such stockings! A woman's dream of stockings! Look: a swallow here,

[*She points to her ankle.*]

a ship here,

[*She points to her calf.*]

and here,

[*She points to her thigh.*]

a rose!

MOTHER-IN-LAW: Child!

GIRL: A rose with the seeds and the stem! Oh! All in silk.

MOTHER-IN-LAW: Two rich families are being brought together.

[LEONARDO *and his* WIFE *appear.*]

GIRL: I came to tell you what they're buying.

LEONARDO [*loudly*]: We don't care.

WIFE: Leave her alone.

MOTHER-IN-LAW: Leonardo, it's not that important.

GIRL: Please excuse me.

[*She leaves, weeping.*]

MOTHER-IN-LAW: Why do you always have to make trouble with people?

LEONARDO: I didn't ask for your opinion.

[*He sits down.*]

MOTHER-IN-LAW: Very well.

[*Pause.*]

WIFE [*to* LEONARDO]: What's the matter with you? What idea've you got boiling there inside your head? Don't leave me like this, not knowing anything.

LEONARDO: Stop that.

WIFE: No. I want you to look at me and tell me.

LEONARDO: Let me alone.

[*He rises.*]

WIFE: Where are you going, love?

LEONARDO [*sharply*]: Can't you shut up?

MOTHER-IN-LAW [*energetically, to her daughter*]: Be quiet!

[LEONARDO *goes out.*]

The baby!

[*She goes into the bedroom and comes out again with the baby in her arms. The* WIFE *has remained standing, unmoving.*]

MOTHER-IN-LAW:

His poor hooves were bleeding,
his long mane was frozen,
and deep in his eyes
stuck a silvery dagger.
Down he went to the river,
Oh, down he went down!
And his blood was running,
Oh, more than the water.

45

WIFE [*turning slowly, as though dreaming*]:

> Carnation, sleep and dream,
> the horse is drinking from the stream.

MOTHER-IN-LAW:

> My rose, asleep now lie
> the horse is starting to cry.

WIFE:

> Lullaby, my baby.

MOTHER-IN-LAW:

> Ay-y-y, for the big horse
> who didn't like water!

WIFE [*dramatically*]:

> Don't come near, don't come in!
> Go away to the mountains!
> Ay-y-y, for the snow-wound
> big horse of the dawn!

MOTHER-IN-LAW [*weeping*]:

> My baby is sleeping...

WIFE [*weeping, as she slowly moves closer*]:

> My baby is resting...

MOTHER-IN-LAW:

> Carnation, sleep and dream,
> the horse won't drink from the stream.

WIFE [*weeping, and leaning on the table*]:

> My rose, asleep now lie,
> the horse is starting to cry.

CURTAIN

ACT ONE

SCENE 3

Interior of the cave where the BRIDE *lives. At the back is a cross of large rose-coloured flowers. The round doors have lace curtains with rose-coloured ties. Around the walls, which are of a white and hard material, are round fans, blue jars, and little mirrors.*

SERVANT: Come right in . . .

[*She is very affable, full of humble hypocrisy. The* BRIDEGROOM *and his* MOTHER *enter. The* MOTHER *is dressed in black satin and wears a lace mantilla; the* BRIDEGROOM *in black corduroy with a great golden chain.*]

Won't you sit down? They'll be right here.

[*She leaves. The* MOTHER *and* SON *are left sitting motionless as statues. Long pause.*]

MOTHER: Did you wear the watch?

BRIDEGROOM: Yes.

[*He takes it out and looks at it.*]

MOTHER: We have to be back on time. How far away these people live!

BRIDEGROOM: But this is good land.

MOTHER: Good; but much too lonesome. A four-hour trip and not one house, not one tree.

BRIDEGROOM: This is the wasteland.

MOTHER: Your father would have covered it with trees.

BRIDEGROOM: Without water?

MOTHER: He would have found some. In the three years we were married he planted ten cherry trees,

[*Remembering*]

those three walnut trees by the mill, a whole vineyard, and a plant called Jupiter which had scarlet flowers – but it dried up.

[*Pause.*]

47

BRIDEGROOM [*referring to the* BRIDE]: She must be dressing.

[*The* BRIDE'S FATHER *enters. He is very old, with shining white hair. His head is bowed. The* MOTHER *and the* BRIDEGROOM *rise. They shake hands in silence.*]

FATHER: Was it a long trip?

MOTHER: Four hours.

[*They sit down.*]

FATHER: You must have come the longest way.

MOTHER: I'm too old to come along the cliffs by the river.

BRIDEGROOM: She gets dizzy.

[*Pause.*]

FATHER: A good hemp harvest.

BRIDEGROOM: A really good one.

FATHER: When I was young this land didn't even grow hemp. We've had to punish it, even weep over it, to make it give us anything useful.

MOTHER: But now it does. Don't complain. I'm not here to ask you for anything.

FATHER [*smiling*]: You're richer than I. Your vineyards are worth a fortune. Each young vine a silver coin. But – do you know? – what bothers me is that our lands are separated. I like to have everything together. One thorn I have in my heart, and that's the little orchard there, stuck in between my fields – and they won't sell it to me for all the gold in the world.

BRIDEGROOM: That's the way it always is.

FATHER: If we could just take twenty teams of oxen and move your vineyards over here, and put them down on that hillside, how happy I'd be!

MOTHER: But why?

FATHER: What's mine is hers and what's yours is his. That's why. Just to see it all together. How beautiful it is to bring things together!

BRIDEGROOM: And it would be less work.

MOTHER: When I die, you could sell ours and buy here, right alongside.

48

FATHER: Sell, sell? Bah! Buy, my friend, buy everything. If I had had sons I would have bought all this mountainside right up to the part with the stream. It's not good land, but strong arms can make it good, and since no people pass by, they don't steal your fruit and you can sleep in peace.

[*Pause.*]

MOTHER: You know what I'm here for.

FATHER: Yes.

MOTHER: And?

FATHER: It seems all right to me. They have talked it over.

MOTHER: My son has money and knows how to manage it.

FATHER: My daughter, too.

MOTHER: My son is handsome. He's never known a woman. His good name cleaner than a sheet spread out in the sun.

FATHER: No need to tell you about my daughter. At three, when the morning star shines, she prepares the bread. She never talks: soft as wool, she embroiders all kinds of fancy work and she can cut a strong cord with her teeth.

MOTHER: God bless her house.

FATHER: May God bless it.

[*The* SERVANT *appears with two trays. One with drinks and the other with sweets.*]

MOTHER [*to the* SON]: When would you like the wedding?

BRIDEGROOM: Next Thursday.

FATHER: The day on which she'll be exactly twenty-two years old.

MOTHER: Twenty-two! My eldest son would be that age if he were alive. Warm and manly as he was, he'd be living now if men hadn't invented knives.

FATHER: One mustn't think about that.

MOTHER: Every minute. Always a hand on your breast.

FATHER: Thursday, then? Is that right?

BRIDEGROOM: That's right.

FATHER: You and I and the bridal couple will go in a carriage to the church which is very far from here; the wedding party on the carts and horses they'll bring with them.

MOTHER: Agreed.

    [*The* SERVANT *passes through.*]

FATHER: Tell her she may come in now.

    [*To the* MOTHER]

  I shall be much pleased if you like her.

    [*The* BRIDE *appears. Her hands fall in a modest pose and her head is bowed.*]

MOTHER: Come here. Are you happy?

BRIDE: Yes, señora.

FATHER: You shouldn't be so solemn. After all, she's going to be your mother.

BRIDE: I'm happy. I've said 'yes' because I wanted to.

MOTHER: Naturally.

    [*She takes her by the chin.*]

  Look at me.

FATHER: She resembles my wife in every way.

MOTHER: Yes? What a beautiful glance! Do you know what it is to be married, child?

BRIDE [*seriously*]: I do.

MOTHER: A man, some children, and a wall two yards thick for everything else.

BRIDEGROOM: Is anything else needed?

MOTHER: No. Just that you all live – that's it! Live long!

BRIDE: I'll know how to keep my word.

MOTHER: Here are some gifts for you.

BRIDE: Thank you.

FATHER: Shall we have something?

MOTHER: Nothing for me.

    [*To the* SON]

  But you?

BRIDEGROOM: Yes, thank you.

    [*He takes one sweet, the* BRIDE *another.*]

FATHER [*to the* BRIDEGROOM]: Wine?

MOTHER: He doesn't touch it.

FATHER: All the better.

[*Pause. All are standing.*]

BRIDEGROOM [*to the* BRIDE]: I'll come tomorrow.

BRIDE: What time?

BRIDEGROOM: Five.

BRIDE: I'll be waiting for you.

BRIDEGROOM: When I leave your side I feel a great emptiness, and something like a knot in my throat.

BRIDE: When you are my husband you won't have it any more.

BRIDEGROOM: That's what I tell myself.

MOTHER: Come. The sun doesn't wait.

[*To the* FATHER]

Are we agreed on everything?

FATHER: Agreed.

MOTHER [*to the* SERVANT]: Good-bye, woman.

SERVANT: God go with you!

[*The* MOTHER *kisses the* BRIDE *and they begin to leave in silence.*]

MOTHER [*at the door*]: Good-bye, daughter.

[*The* BRIDE *answers with her hand.*]

FATHER: I'll go out with you.

[*They leave.*]

SERVANT: I'm bursting to see the presents.

BRIDE [*sharply*]: Stop that!

SERVANT: Oh, child, show them to me.

BRIDE: I don't want to.

SERVANT: At least the stockings. They say they're all open work. Please!

BRIDE: I said no.

SERVANT: Well, my Lord. All right then. It looks as if you didn't want to get married.

BRIDE [*biting her hand in anger*]: Ay-y-y!

SERVANT: Child, child! What's the matter with you? Are you sorry to give up your queen's life? Don't think of bitter things. Have you any reason to? None. Let's look at the presents.

[*She takes the box.*]

BRIDE [*holding her by the wrists*]: Let go.

SERVANT: Ay-y-y, girl!

BRIDE: Let go, I said.

SERVANT: You're stronger than a man.

BRIDE: Haven't I done a man's work? I wish I were.

SERVANT: Don't talk like that.

BRIDE: Quiet, I said. Let's talk about something else.

[*The light is fading from the stage. Long pause.*]

SERVANT: Did you hear a horse last night?

BRIDE: What time?

SERVANT: Three.

BRIDE: It might have been a stray horse – from the herd.

SERVANT: No. It carried a rider.

BRIDE: How do you know?

SERVANT: Because I saw him. He was standing by your window. It shocked me greatly.

BRIDE: Maybe it was my fiancé. Sometimes he comes by at that time.

SERVANT: No.

BRIDE: You saw him?

SERVANT: Yes.

BRIDE: Who was it?

SERVANT: It was Leonardo.

BRIDE [*strongly*]: Liar! You liar! Why should he come here?

SERVANT: He came.

BRIDE: Shut up! Shut your cursed mouth.

[*The sound of a horse is heard.*]

SERVANT [*at the window*]: Look. Lean out. Was it Leonardo?

BRIDE: It was!

QUICK CURTAIN

ACT TWO

SCENE I

The entrance hall of the BRIDE'S *house. A large door in the back. It is night.*
[The BRIDE *enters wearing ruffled white petticoats full of laces and*
embroidered bands, and a sleeveless white bodice. The SERVANT *is*
dressed the same way.]

SERVANT: I'll finish combing your hair out here.

BRIDE: It's too warm to stay in there.

SERVANT: In this country it doesn't even cool off at dawn.

[The BRIDE *sits on a low chair and looks into a little hand mirror. The*
SERVANT *combs her hair.]*

BRIDE: My mother came from a place with lots of trees – from a
fertile country.

SERVANT: And she was so happy!

BRIDE: But she wasted away here.

SERVANT: Fate.

BRIDE: As we're all wasting away here. The very walls give off heat.
Ay-y-y! Don't pull so hard.

SERVANT: I'm only trying to fix this wave better. I want it to fall
over your forehead.

[The BRIDE *looks at herself in the mirror.]*

How beautiful you are! Ay-y-y!

[She kisses her passionately.]

BRIDE [*seriously*]: Keep right on combing.

SERVANT [*combing*]: Oh, lucky you – going to put your arms around
a man; and kiss him; and feel his weight.

BRIDE: Hush.

SERVANT: And the best part will be when you'll wake up and you'll
feel him at your side and when he caresses your shoulders with his
breath, like a little nightingale's feather!

BRIDE [*sternly*]: Will you be quiet.

53

SERVANT: But, child! What *is* a wedding? A wedding is just that and nothing more. Is it the sweets – or the bouquets of flowers? No. It's a shining bed and a man and a woman.

BRIDE: But you shouldn't talk about it.

SERVANT: Oh, *that's* something else again. But fun enough too.

BRIDE: Or bitter enough.

SERVANT: I'm going to put the orange blossoms on from here to here, so the wreath will shine out on top of your hair.

[*She tries on the sprigs of orange blossom.*]

BRIDE [*looking at herself in the mirror*]: Give it to me.

[*She takes the wreath, looks at it, and lets her head fall in discouragement.*]

SERVANT: Now what's the matter?

BRIDE: Leave me alone.

SERVANT: This is no time for you to start feeling sad.

[*Encouragingly*]

Give me the wreath.

[*The BRIDE takes the wreath and hurls it away.*]

Child! You're just asking God to punish you, throwing the wreath on the floor like that. Raise your head! Don't you want to get married? Say it. You can still withdraw.

[*The BRIDE rises.*]

BRIDE: Storm clouds. A chill wind that cuts through my heart. Who hasn't felt it?

SERVANT: You love your sweetheart, don't you?

BRIDE: I love him.

SERVANT: Yes, yes. I'm sure you do.

BRIDE: But this is a very serious step.

SERVANT: You've got to take it.

BRIDE: I've already given my word.

SERVANT: I'll put on the wreath.

BRIDE [*she sits down*]: Hurry. They should be arriving by now.

SERVANT: They've already been at least two hours on the way.

BRIDE: How far is it from here to the church?

SERVANT: Five leagues by the stream, but twice that by the road.

[*The* BRIDE *rises and the* SERVANT *grows excited as she looks at her.*]

SERVANT:

> Awake, O Bride, awaken,
> On your wedding morning waken!
> The world's rivers may all
> Bear along your bridal Crown!

BRIDE [*smiling*]: Come now.

SERVANT [*enthusiastically kissing her and dancing around her*]:

> Awake,
> with the fresh bouquet
> of flowering laurel.
> Awake,
> by the trunk and branch
> of the laurels!

[*The banging of the front door latch is heard.*]

BRIDE: Open the door! That must be the first guests.

[*She leaves. The* SERVANT *opens the door.*]

SERVANT [*in astonishment*]: You!

LEONARDO: Yes, me. Good morning.

SERVANT: The first one!

LEONARDO: Wasn't I invited?

SERVANT: Yes.

LEONARDO: That's why I'm here.

SERVANT: Where's your wife?

LEONARDO: I came on my horse. She's coming by the road.

SERVANT: Didn't you meet anyone?

LEONARDO: I *passed* them on my horse.

SERVANT: You're going to kill that horse with so much racing.

LEONARDO: When he dies, he's dead!

[*Pause.*]

SERVANT: Sit down. Nobody's up yet.

LEONARDO: Where's the bride?

SERVANT: I'm just on my way to dress her.

LEONARDO: The bride! She ought to be happy!

SERVANT [*changing the subject*]: How's the baby?

LEONARDO: What baby?

SERVANT: Your son.

LEONARDO [*remembering, as though in a dream*]: Ah!

SERVANT: Are they bringing him?

LEONARDO: No.

[*Pause. Voices sing distantly.*]

VOICES:

Awake, O Bride, awaken,
On your wedding morning waken!

LEONARDO:

Awake, O Bride, awaken,
On your wedding morning waken!

SERVANT: It's the guests. They're still quite a way off.

LEONARDO: The bride's going to wear a big wreath, isn't she? But it ought not to be so large. One a little smaller would look better on her. Has the groom already brought her the orange blossom that must be worn on the breast?

BRIDE [*appearing, still in petticoats and wearing the wreath*]: He brought it.

SERVANT [*sternly*]: Don't come out like that.

BRIDE: What does it matter?

[*Seriously*]

Why do you ask if they brought the orange blossom? Do you have something in mind?

LEONARDO: Nothing. What would I have in mind?

[*Drawing near her*]

You, you know me; you know I don't. Tell me so. What have I ever meant to you? Open your memory, refresh it. But two oxen and an ugly little hut are almost nothing. That's the thorn.

BRIDE: What have you come here to do?

LEONARDO: To see your wedding.

BRIDE: Just as I saw yours!

LEONARDO: Tied up by you, done with your two hands. Oh, they can kill me but they can't spit on me. But even money, which shines so much, spits sometimes.

BRIDE: Liar!

LEONARDO: I don't want to talk. I'm hot-blooded and I don't want to shout so all these hills will hear me.

BRIDE: My shouts would be louder.

SERVANT: You'll have to stop talking like this.

[*To the* BRIDE]

You don't have to talk about what's past.

[*The* SERVANT *looks around uneasily at the doors.*]

BRIDE: She's right. I shouldn't even talk to you. But it offends me to the soul that you come here to watch me, and spy on my wedding, and ask about the orange blossom with something on your mind. Go and wait for your wife at the door.

LEONARDO: But, can't you and I even talk?

SERVANT [*with rage*]: No. No, you can't talk.

LEONARDO: Ever since I got married I've been thinking night and day about whose fault it was, and every time I think about it, out comes a new fault to eat up the old one; but always there's a fault left.

BRIDE: A man with a horse knows a lot of things and can do a lot to ride roughshod over a girl stuck out in the desert. But I have my pride. And that's why I'm getting married. I'll lock myself in with my husband and then I'll have to love him above everyone else.

LEONARDO: Pride won't help you a bit.

[*He draws near to her.*]

BRIDE: Don't come near me!

LEONARDO: To burn with desire and keep quiet about it is the greatest punishment we can bring on ourselves. What good was pride to me – and not seeing you, and letting you lie awake night after night? No good! It only served to bring the fire down on me! You think that time heals and walls hide things, but it isn't true, it isn't true! When things get that deep inside you there isn't anybody can change them.

BRIDE [*trembling*]: I can't listen to you. I can't listen to your voice. It's as though I'd drunk a bottle of anise and fallen asleep wrapped

in a quilt of roses. It pulls me along, and I know I'm drowning –
but I go on down.

SERVANT [*seizing* LEONARDO *by the lapels*]: You've got to go right
now!

LEONARDO: This is the last time I'll ever talk to her. Don't you be
afraid of anything.

BRIDE: And I know I'm crazy and I know my breast rots with
longing; but here I am – calmed by hearing him, by just seeing
him move his arms.

LEONARDO: I'd never be at peace if I didn't tell you these things. I
got married. Now you get married.

SERVANT: But she *is* getting married!

[VOICES *are heard singing, nearer.*]

VOICES:

Awake, O Bride, awaken,
On your wedding morning waken!

BRIDE:

Awake, O Bride, awaken.

[*She goes out, running toward her room.*]

SERVANT: The people are here now.

[*To* LEONARDO]

Don't you come near her again.

LEONARDO: Don't worry.

[*He goes out to the left. Day begins to break.*]

FIRST GIRL [*entering*]:

Awake, O Bride, awaken,
the morning you're to marry;
sing round and dance round;
balconies a wreath must carry.

VOICES:

Bride, awaken!

SERVANT [*creating enthusiasm*]:

Awake,
with the green bouquet
of love in flower.

      Awake,
      by the trunk and the branch
      of the laurels!

SECOND GIRL [*entering*]:
      Awake,
      with her long hair,
      snowy sleeping gown,
      patent leather boots with silver –
      her forehead jasmines crown.

SERVANT:
      Oh, shepherdess,
      the moon begins to shine!

FIRST GIRL:
      Oh, gallant,
      leave your hat beneath the vine!

FIRST YOUNG MAN [*entering, holding his hat on high*]:
      Bride, awaken,
      for over the fields
      the wedding draws nigh
      with trays heaped with dahlias
      and cakes piled high.

VOICES:
      Bride, awaken!

SECOND GIRL:
      The bride
      has set her white wreath in place
      and the groom
      ties it on with a golden lace.

SERVANT:
      By the orange tree,
      sleepless the bride will be.

THIRD GIRL [*entering*]:
      By the citron vine,
      gifts from the groom will shine.

    [THREE GUESTS *come in.*]

FIRST YOUTH:

> Dove, awaken!
> In the dawn
> shadowy bells are shaken.

GUEST:

> The bride, the white bride,
> today a maiden,
> tomorrow a wife.

FIRST GIRL:

> Dark one, come down
> trailing the train of your silken gown.

GUEST:

> Little dark one, come down,
> cold morning wears a dewy crown.

FIRST GUEST:

> Awaken, wife, awake,
> orange blossoms the breezes shake.

SERVANT:

> A tree I would embroider her
> with garnet sashes wound,
> And on each sash a cupid,
> with 'Long Live' all around.

VOICES:

> Bride, awaken.

FIRST YOUTH:

> The morning you're to marry!

GUEST:

> The morning you're to marry
> how elegant you'll seem;
> worthy, mountain flower,
> of a captain's dream.

FATHER [entering]:

> A captain's wife
> the groom will marry.
> He comes with his oxen the treasure to carry!

60

THIRD GIRL:

> The groom
> is like a flower of gold.
> When he walks,
> blossoms at his feet unfold.

SERVANT:

> Oh, my lucky girl!

SECOND YOUTH:

> Bride, awaken.

SERVANT:

> Oh, my elegant girl!

FIRST GIRL:

> Through the windows
> hear the wedding shout.

SECOND GIRL:

> Let the bride come out.

FIRST GIRL:

> Come out, come out!

SERVANT:

> Let the bells
> ring and ring out clear!

FIRST YOUTH:

> For here she comes!
> For now she's near!

SERVANT:

> Like a bull, the wedding
> is arising here!

[*The* BRIDE *appears. She wears a black dress in the style of 1900, with a bustle and large train covered with pleated gauzes and heavy laces. Upon her hair, brushed in a wave over her forehead, she wears an orange-blossom wreath. Guitars sound. The* GIRLS *kiss the* BRIDE.]

THIRD GIRL: What scent did you put on your hair?

BRIDE [*laughing*]: None at all.

SECOND GIRL [*looking at her dress*]: This cloth is what you can't get.

FIRST YOUTH: Here's the groom!

BRIDEGROOM: Salud!

FIRST GIRL [*putting a flower behind his ear*]:

> The groom
> is like a flower of gold.

SECOND GIRL:

> Quiet breezes
> from his eyes unfold.

[*The* GROOM *goes to the* BRIDE.]

BRIDE: Why did you put on those shoes?

BRIDEGROOM: They're gayer than the black ones.

LEONARDO'S WIFE [*entering and kissing the* BRIDE]: Salud!

[*They all speak excitedly.*]

LEONARDO [*entering as one who performs a duty*]:

> The morning you're to marry
> We give you a wreath to wear.

LEONARDO'S WIFE:

> So the fields may be made happy
> with the dew dropped from your hair!

MOTHER [*to the* FATHER]: Are those people here, too?

FATHER: They're part of the family. Today is a day of forgiveness!

MOTHER: I'll put up with it, but I don't forgive.

BRIDEGROOM: With your wreath, it's a joy to look at you!

BRIDE: Let's go to the church quickly.

BRIDEGROOM: Are you in a hurry?

BRIDE: Yes. I want to be your wife right now so that I can be with you alone, not hearing any voice but yours.

BRIDEGROOM: That's what I want!

BRIDE: And not seeing any eyes but yours. And for you to hug me so hard, that even though my dead mother should call me, I wouldn't be able to draw away from you.

BRIDEGROOM: My arms are strong. I'll hug you for forty years without stopping.

BRIDE [*taking his arm, dramatically*]: For ever!

FATHER: Quick now! Round up the teams and carts! The sun's already out.

MOTHER: And go along carefully! Let's hope nothing goes wrong.

[*The great door in the background opens.*]

SERVANT [*weeping*]:

> As you set out from your house,
> oh, maiden white,
> remember you leave shining
> with a star's light.

FIRST GIRL:

> Clean of body, clean of clothes
> from her home to church she goes.

[*They start leaving.*]

SECOND GIRL:

> Now you leave your home
> for the church!

SERVANT:

> The wind sets flowers
> on the sands.

THIRD GIRL:

> Ah, the white maid!

SERVANT:

> Dark winds are the lace
> of her mantilla.

[*They leave. Guitars, castanets, and tambourines are heard. LEO-NARDO and his WIFE are left alone.*]

WIFE: Let's go.

LEONARDO: Where?

WIFE: To the church. But not on your horse. You're coming with me.

LEONARDO: In the cart?

WIFE: Is there anything else?

LEONARDO: I'm not the kind of man to ride in a cart.

WIFE: Nor I the wife to go to a wedding without her husband. I can't stand any more of this!

LEONARDO: Neither can I!

WIFE: And why do you look at me that way? With a thorn in each eye.

LEONARDO: Let's go!

WIFE: I don't know what's happening. But I think, and I don't want to think. One thing I do know. I'm already cast off by you. But I have a son. And another coming. And so it goes. My mother's fate was the same. Well, I'm not moving from here.

[VOICES *outside*.]

VOICES:

> As you set out from your home
> and to the church go,
> remember you leave shining
> with a star's glow.

WIFE [*weeping*]:

> Remember you leave shining
> with a star's glow.

I left my house like that too. They could have stuffed the whole countryside in my mouth. I was that trusting.

LEONARDO [*rising*]: Let's go!

WIFE: But you with me!

LEONARDO: Yes.

[*Pause.*]

Start moving!

[*They leave.*]

VOICES:

> As you set out from your home
> and to the church go,
> remember you leave shining
> with a star's glow.

SLOW CURTAIN

ACT TWO

SCENE 2

The exterior of the BRIDE's *Cave Home, in white, grey, and cold blue tones. Large cactus trees. Shadowy and silver tones. Panoramas of light tan tablelands, everything hard like a landscape in popular ceramics.*

SERVANT [*arranging glasses and trays on a table*]:
>A-turning,
>the wheel was a-turning
>and the water was flowing,
>for the wedding night comes.
>May the branches part
>and the moon be arrayed
>at her white balcony rail.

[*In a loud voice*]
Set out the tablecloths!

[*In a pathetic voice*]
>A-singing,
>bride and groom were singing
>and the water was flowing
>for their wedding night comes.
>Oh, rime-frost, flash! –
>and almonds bitter
>fill with honey!

[*In a loud voice*]
Get the wine ready!

[*In a poetic tone*]
>Elegant girl,
>most elegant in the world,
>see the way the water is flowing,
>for your wedding night comes.
>Hold your skirts close in

under the bridegroom's wing
and never leave your house,
for the bridegroom is a dove
with his breast a firebrand
and the fields wait for the whisper
of spurting blood.
A-turning
the wheel was a-turning
and the water was flowing
and your wedding night comes.
Oh, water, sparkle!

MOTHER [*entering*]: At last!

FATHER: Are we the first ones?

SERVANT: No, Leonardo and his wife arrived a while ago. They drove like demons. His wife got here dead with fright. They made the trip as though they'd come on horseback.

FATHER: That one's looking for trouble. He's not of good blood.

MOTHER: What blood would you expect him to have? His whole family's blood. It comes down from his great-grandfather, who started in killing, and it goes on down through the whole evil breed of knife-wielding and false-smiling men.

FATHER: Let's leave it at that!

SERVANT: But how can she leave it at that?

MOTHER: It hurts me to the tips of my veins. On the forehead of all of them I see only the hand with which they killed what was mine. Can you really see me? Don't I seem mad to you? Well, it's the madness of not having shrieked out all my breast needs to. Always in my breast there's a shriek standing tiptoe that I have to beat down and hold in under my shawls. But the dead are carried off and one has to keep still. And then, people find fault.

[*She removes her shawl.*]

FATHER: Today's not the day for you to be remembering these things.

MOTHER: When the talk turns on it, I have to speak. And more so today. Because today I'm left alone in my house.

FATHER: But with the expectation of having someone with you.

MOTHER: That's my hope: grandchildren.

[*They sit down.*]

FATHER: I want them to have a lot of them. This land needs hands that aren't hired. There's a battle to be waged against weeds, the thistles, the big rocks that come from one doesn't know where. And those hands have to be the owner's, who chastises and dominates, who makes the seeds grow. Lots of sons are needed.

MOTHER: And some daughters! Men are like the wind! They're forced to handle weapons. Girls never go out into the street.

FATHER [*happily*]: I think they'll have both.

MOTHER: My son will cover her well. He's of good seed. His father could have had many sons with me.

FATHER: What I'd like is to have all this happen in a day. So that right away they'd have two or three boys.

MOTHER: But it's not like that. It takes a long time. That's why it's so terrible to see one's own blood spilled out on the ground. A fountain that spurts for a minute, but costs us years. When I got to my son, he lay fallen in the middle of the street. I wet my hands with his blood and licked them with my tongue – because it was my blood. You don't know what that's like. In a glass and topaz shrine I'd put the earth moistened by his blood.

FATHER: Now you must hope. My daughter is wide-hipped and your son is strong.

MOTHER: That's why I'm hoping.

[*They rise.*]

FATHER: Get the wheat trays ready!

SERVANT: They're all ready.

LEONARDO'S WIFE [*entering*]: May it be for the best!

MOTHER: Thank you.

LEONARDO: Is there going to be a celebration?

FATHER: A small one. People can't stay long.

SERVANT: Here they are!

[GUESTS *begin entering in gay groups. The* BRIDE *and* GROOM *come in arm-in-arm.* LEONARDO *leaves.*[

BRIDEGROOM: There's never been a wedding with so many peopl

BRIDE [*sullen*]: Never.

FATHER: It was brilliant.

MOTHER: Whole branches of families came.

BRIDEGROOM: People who never went out of the house.

MOTHER: Your father sowed well, and now you're reaping it.

BRIDEGROOM: There were cousins of mine whom I no longer knew.

MOTHER: All the people from the seacoast.

BRIDEGROOM [*happily*]: They were frightened of the horses.

[*They talk.*]

MOTHER [*to the* BRIDE]: What are you thinking about?

BRIDE: I'm not thinking about anything.

MOTHER: Your blessings weigh heavily.

[*Guitars are heard.*]

BRIDE: Like lead.

MOTHER [*stern*]: But they shouldn't weigh so. Happy as a dove you
ought to be.

BRIDE: Are you staying here tonight?

MOTHER: No. My house is empty.

BRIDE: You ought to stay!

FATHER [*to the* MOTHER]: Look at the dance they're forming. Dances
of the far-away seashore.

[LEONARDO *enters and sits down. His* WIFE *stands rigidly behind
him.*]

MOTHER: They're my husband's cousins. Stiff as stones at dancing.

FATHER: It makes me happy to watch them. What a change for this
house!

[*He leaves.*]

BRIDEGROOM [*to the* BRIDE]: Did you like the orange blossom?

BRIDE [*looking at him fixedly*]: Yes.

BRIDEGROOM: It's all of wax. It will last for ever. I'd like you to
have had them all over your dress.

BRIDE: No need of that.

[LEONARDO *goes off to the right.*]

FIRST GIRL: Let's go and take out your pins.

BRIDE [*to the* GROOM]: I'll be right back.

LEONARDO'S WIFE: I hope you'll be happy with my cousin!

BRIDEGROOM: I'm sure I will.

LEONARDO'S WIFE: The two of you here; never going out; building a home. I wish I could live far away like this, too!

BRIDEGROOM: Why don't you buy land? The mountainside is cheap and children grow up better.

LEONARDO'S WIFE: We don't have any money. And at the rate we're going . . . !

BRIDEGROOM: Your husband is a good worker.

LEONARDO'S WIFE: Yes, but he likes to fly around too much; from one thing to another. He's not a patient man.

SERVANT: Aren't you having anything? I'm going to wrap up some wine cakes for your mother. She likes them so much.

BRIDEGROOM: Put up three dozen for her.

LEONARDO'S WIFE: No, no. A half-dozen's enough for her!

BRIDEGROOM: But today's a day!

LEONARDO'S WIFE [*to the* SERVANT]: Where's Leonardo?

BRIDEGROOM: He must be with the guests.

LEONARDO'S WIFE: I'm going to go see.

[*She leaves.*]

SERVANT [*looking off at the dance*]: That's beautiful there.

BRIDEGROOM: Aren't you dancing?

SERVANT: No one will ask me.

[TWO GIRLS *pass across the back of the stage; during this whole scene the background should be an animated crossing of figures.*]

BRIDEGROOM [*happily*]: They just don't know anything. Lively old girls like you dance better than the young ones.

SERVANT: Well! Are you tossing me a compliment, boy? What a family yours is! Men among men! As a little girl I saw your grandfather's wedding. What a figure! It seemed as if a mountain were getting married.

BRIDEGROOM: I'm not as tall.

SERVANT: But there's the same twinkle in your eye. Where's the girl?

BRIDEGROOM: Taking off her wreath.

SERVANT: Ah! Look. For midnight, since you won't be sleeping, I have prepared ham for you, and some large glasses of old wine. On the lower shelf of the cupboard. In case you need it.

BRIDEGROOM [*smiling*]: I won't be eating at midnight.

SERVANT [*slyly*]: If not you, maybe the bride.

   [*She leaves.*]

FIRST YOUTH [*entering*]: You've got to come have a drink with us!

BRIDEGROOM: I'm waiting for the bride.

SECOND YOUTH: You'll have her at dawn!

FIRST YOUTH: That's when it's best!

SECOND YOUTH: Just for a minute.

BRIDEGROOM: Let's go.

   [*They leave. Great excitement is heard. The* BRIDE *enters. From the opposite side* TWO GIRLS *come running to meet her.*]

FIRST GIRL: To whom did you give the first pin; me or this one?

BRIDE: I don't remember.

FIRST GIRL: To me, you gave it to me here.

SECOND GIRL: To me, in front of the altar.

BRIDE [*uneasily, with a great inner struggle*]: I don't know anything about it.

FIRST GIRL: It's just that I wish you'd . . .

BRIDE [*interrupting*]: Nor do I care. I have a lot to think about.

SECOND GIRL: Your pardon.

   [LEONARDO *crosses at the rear of the stage.*]

BRIDE [*she sees* LEONARDO]: And this is an upsetting time.

FIRST GIRL: We wouldn't know anything about that!

BRIDE: You'll know about it when your time comes. This step is a very hard one to take.

FIRST GIRL: Has she offended you?

BRIDE: No. You must pardon me.

SECOND GIRL: What for? But *both* the pins are good for getting married, aren't they?

BRIDE: Both of them.

FIRST GIRL: Maybe now one will get married before the other.

BRIDE: Are you so eager?

SECOND GIRL [*shyly*]: Yes.

BRIDE: Why?

FIRST GIRL: Well . . .

[*She embraces the* SECOND GIRL. *Both go running off. The* GROOM *comes in very slowly and embraces the* BRIDE *from behind.*]

BRIDE [*in sudden fright*]: Let go of me!

BRIDEGROOM: Are you frightened of me?

BRIDE: Ay-y-y! It's you?

BRIDEGROOM: Who else would it be?

[*Pause.*]

  Your father or me.

BRIDE: That's true!

BRIDEGROOM: Of course, your father would have hugged you more gently.

BRIDE [*darkly*]: Of course!

BRIDEGROOM [*embracing her strongly and a little bit brusquely*]: Because he's old.

BRIDE [*curtly*]: Let me go!

BRIDEGROOM: Why?

[*He lets her go.*]

BRIDE: Well . . . the people. They can see us.

[*The* SERVANT *crosses at the back of the stage again without looking at the* BRIDE *and* BRIDEGROOM.]

BRIDEGROOM: What of it? It's consecrated now.

BRIDE: Yes, but let me be . . . Later.

BRIDEGROOM: What's the matter with you? You look frightened!

BRIDE: I'm all right. Don't go.

[LEONARDO'S WIFE *enters.*]

LEONARDO'S WIFE: I don't mean to intrude . . .

BRIDEGROOM: What is it?

LEONARDO'S WIFE: Did my husband come through here?

BRIDEGROOM: No.

LEONARDO'S WIFE: Because I can't find him, and his horse isn't in the stable either.

BRIDEGROOM [*happily*]: He must be out racing it.

[*The* WIFE *leaves, troubled. The* SERVANT *enters.*]

SERVANT: Aren't you two proud and happy with so many good wishes?

BRIDEGROOM: I wish it were over with. The bride is a little tired.

SERVANT: That's no way to act, child.

BRIDE: It's as though I'd been struck on the head.

SERVANT: A bride from these mountains must be strong.

[*To the* GROOM]

You're the only one who can cure her, because she's yours.

[*She goes running off.*]

BRIDEGROOM [*embracing the* BRIDE]: Let's go dance a little.

[*He kisses her.*]

BRIDE [*worried*]: No. I'd like to stretch out on my bed a little.

BRIDEGROOM: I'll keep you company.

BRIDE: Never! With all these people here? What would they say? Let me be quiet for a moment.

BRIDEGROOM: Whatever you say! But don't be like that tonight!

BRIDE [*at the door*]: I'll be better tonight.

BRIDEGROOM: That's what I want.

[*The* MOTHER *appears.*]

MOTHER: Son.

BRIDEGROOM: Where've you been?

MOTHER: Out there – in all that noise. Are you happy?

BRIDEGROOM: Yes.

MOTHER: Where's your wife?

BRIDEGROOM: Resting a little. It's a bad day for brides!

MOTHER: A bad day? The only good one. To me it was like coming into my own.

[*The* SERVANT *enters and goes toward the* BRIDE's *room.*]

Like the breaking of new ground; the planting of new trees.

BRIDEGROOM: Are you going to leave?

MOTHER: Yes, I ought to be at home.

BRIDEGROOM: Alone.

MOTHER: Not alone. For my head is full of things: of men, and fights.

BRIDEGROOM: But now the fights are no longer fights.

[*The* SERVANT *enters quickly; she disappears at the rear of the stage, running.*]

MOTHER: While you live, you have to fight.

BRIDEGROOM. I'll always obey you!

MOTHER: Try to be loving with your wife, and if you see she's acting foolish or touchy, caress her in a way that will hurt her a little: a strong hug, a bite, and then a soft kiss. Not so she'll be angry, but just so she'll feel you're the man, the boss, the one who gives orders. I learned that from your father. And since you don't have him, I have to be the one to tell you about these strong defences.

BRIDEGROOM: I'll always do as you say.

FATHER [*entering*]: Where's my daughter?

BRIDEGROOM: She's inside.

[*The* FATHER *goes to look for her.*]

FIRST GIRL: Get the bride and groom! We're going to dance a round!

FIRST YOUTH [*to the* BRIDEGROOM]: You're going to lead it.

FATHER [*entering*]: She's not there.

BRIDEGROOM: No?

FATHER: She must have gone up to the railing.

BRIDEGROOM: I'll go see!

[*He leaves. A hubbub of excitement and guitars is heard.*]

FIRST GIRL: They've started it already!

[*She leaves.*]

BRIDEGROOM [*entering*]: She isn't there.

MOTHER [*uneasily*]: Isn't she?

FATHER: But where could she have gone?

SERVANT [*entering*]: But where's the girl, where is she?

MOTHER [*seriously*]: That we don't know.

[*The* BRIDEGROOM *leaves.* THREE GUESTS *enter.*]

FATHER [*dramatically*]: But, isn't she in the dance?

SERVANT: She's not in the dance.

FATHER [*with a start*]: There are a lot of people. Go look!

SERVANT: I've already looked.

FATHER [*tragically*]: Then where is she?

BRIDEGROOM [*entering*]: Nowhere. Not anywhere.

MOTHER [*to the* FATHER]: What does this mean? Where is your daughter?

    [LEONARDO'S WIFE *enters*.]

LEONARDO'S WIFE: They've run away! They've run away! She and Leonardo. On the horse. With their arms around each other, they rode off like a shooting star!

FATHER: That's not true! Not my daughter!

MOTHER: Yes, your daughter! Spawn of a wicked mother, and he, he too. But now she's my son's wife!

BRIDEGROOM [*entering*]: Let's go after them! Who has a horse?

MOTHER: Who has a horse? Right away! Who has a horse? I'll give him all I have – my eyes, my tongue even. . . .

VOICE: Here's one.

MOTHER [*to the* SON]: Go! After them!

    [*He leaves with two young men.*]

No. Don't go. Those people kill quickly and well . . . but yes, run, and I'll follow!

FATHER: It couldn't be my daughter. Perhaps she's thrown herself in the well.

MOTHER: Decent women throw themselves in water; not that one! But now she's my son's wife. Two groups. There are two groups here.

    [*They all enter.*]

My family and yours. Everyone set out from here. Shake the dust from your heels! We'll go help my son.

    [*The people separate into two groups.*]

For he has his family: his cousins from the sea, and all who came from inland. Out of here! On all roads. The hour of blood has come again. Two groups! You with yours and I with mine. After them! After them!

CURTAIN

ACT THREE

SCENE I

A forest. It is night-time. Great moist tree trunks. A dark atmosphere. Two violins are heard.

   [THREE WOODCUTTERS *enter.*]

FIRST WOODCUTTER: And have they found them?

SECOND WOODCUTTER: No. But they're looking for them everywhere.

THIRD WOODCUTTER: They'll find them.

SECOND WOODCUTTER: Sh-h-h!

THIRD WOODCUTTER: What?

SECOND WOODCUTTER: They seem to be coming closer on all the roads at once.

FIRST WOODCUTTER: When the moon comes out they'll see them.

SECOND WOODCUTTER: They ought to let them go.

FIRST WOODCUTTER: The world is wide. Everybody can live in it.

THIRD WOODCUTTER: But they'll kill them.

SECOND WOODCUTTER: You have to follow your passion. They did right to run away.

FIRST WOODCUTTER: They were deceiving themselves but at the last blood was stronger.

THIRD WOODCUTTER: Blood!

FIRST WOODCUTTER: You have to follow the path of your blood.

SECOND WOODCUTTER: But blood that sees the light of day is drunk up by the earth.

FIRST WOODCUTTER: What of it? Better dead with the blood drained away than alive with it rotting.

THIRD WOODCUTTER: Hush!

FIRST WOODCUTTER: What? Do you hear something?

THIRD WOODCUTTER: I hear the crickets, the frogs, the night's ambush.

75

FIRST WOODCUTTER: But not the horse.

THIRD WOODCUTTER: No.

FIRST WOODCUTTER: By now he must be loving her.

SECOND WOODCUTTER: Her body for him; his body for her.

THIRD WOODCUTTER: They'll find them and they'll kill them.

FIRST WOODCUTTER: But by then they'll have mingled their bloods. They'll be like two empty jars, like two dry arroyos.

SECOND WOODCUTTER: There are many clouds and it would be easy for the moon not to come out.

THIRD WOODCUTTER: The bridegroom will find them with or without the moon. I saw him set out. Like a raging star. His face the colour of ashes. He looked the fate of all his clan.

FIRST WOODCUTTER: His clan of dead men lying in the middle of the street.

SECOND WOODCUTTER: There you have it!

THIRD WOODCUTTER: You think they'll be able to break through the circle?

SECOND WOODCUTTER: It's hard to. There are knives and guns for ten leagues round.

THIRD WOODCUTTER: He's riding a good horse.

SECOND WOODCUTTER: But he's carrying a woman.

FIRST WOODCUTTER: We're close by now.

SECOND WOODCUTTER: A tree with forty branches. We'll soon cut it down.

THIRD WOODCUTTER: The moon's coming out now. Let's hurry.

[*From the left shines a brightness.*]

FIRST WOODCUTTER:

    O rising moon!
    Moon among the great leaves.

SECOND WOODCUTTER:

    Cover the blood with jasmines!

FIRST WOODCUTTER:

    O lonely moon!
    Moon among the great leaves.

SECOND WOODCUTTER:

    Silver on the bride's face.

THIRD WOODCUTTER:

    O evil moon!

    Leave for their love a branch in shadow.

FIRST WOODCUTTER:

    O sorrowing moon!

    Leave for their love a branch in shadow.

[*They go out. The* MOON *appears through a shining brightness at the left. The* MOON *is a young woodcutter with a white face. The stage takes on an intense blue radiance.*]

MOON:

    Round swan in the river
    and a cathedral's eye,
    false dawn on the leaves,
    they'll not escape; these things am I!
    Who is hiding? And who sobs
    in the thornbrakes of the valley?
    The moon sets a knife
    abandoned in the air
    which being a leaden threat
    yearns to be blood's pain.
    Let me in! I come freezing
    down to walls and windows!
    Open roofs, open breasts
    where I may warm myself!
    I'm cold! My ashes
    of somnolent metals
    seek the fire's crest
    on mountains and streets.
    But the snow carries me
    upon its mottled back
    and pools soak me
    in their water, hard and cold.
    But this night there will be

red blood for my cheeks,
and for the reeds that cluster
at the wide feet of the wind.
Let there be neither shadow nor bower,
and then they can't get away!
O let me enter a breast
where I may get warm!
A heart for me!
Warm! That will spurt
over the mountains of my chest;
let me come in, oh let me!

[*To the branches*]

I want no shadows. My rays
must get in everywhere,
even among the dark trunks I want
the whisper of gleaming lights,
so that this night there will be
sweet blood for my cheeks,
and for the needs that cluster
at the wide feet of the wind.
Who is hiding? Out, I say!
No! They will not get away!
I will light up the horse
with a fever bright as diamonds.

[*He disappears among the trunks, and the stage goes back to its dark lighting. An* OLD WOMAN *comes out completely covered by thin green cloth. She is barefooted. Her face can barely be seen among the folds. This character does not appear in the cast.*]

BEGGAR WOMAN:

That moon's going away, just when they's near.
They won't get past here. The river's whisper
and the whispering tree trunks will muffle
the torn flight of their shrieks.
It has to be here, and soon. I'm worn out.
The coffins are ready, and white sheets

wait on the floor of the bedroom
for heavy bodies with torn throats.
Let not one bird awake, let the breeze,
gathering their moans in her skirt,
fly with them over black tree-tops
or bury them in soft mud.

[*Impatiently*]

Oh, that moon! That moon!

[*The* MOON *appears. The intense blue light returns.*]

MOON: They're coming. One band through the ravine and the other along the river. I'm going to light up the boulders. What do you need?

BEGGAR WOMAN: Nothing.

MOON: The wind blows hard now, with a double edge.

BEGGAR WOMAN: Light up the waistcoat and open the buttons; the knives will know the path after that.

MOON:

But let them be a long time a-dying. So the blood
will slide its delicate hissing between my fingers.
Look how my ashen valleys already are waking
in longing for this fountain of shuddering gushes!

BEGGAR WOMAN: Let's not let them get past the arroyo. Silence!

MOON: There they come!

[*He goes. The stage is left dark.*]

BEGGAR WOMAN: Quick! Lots of light! Do you hear me? They can't get away!

[*The* BRIDEGROOM *and the* FIRST YOUTH *enter. The* BEGGAR WOMAN *sits down and covers herself with her cloak.*]

BRIDEGROOM: This way.

FIRST YOUTH: You won't find them.

BRIDEGROOM [*angrily*]: Yes, I'll find them.

FIRST YOUTH: I think they've taken another path.

BRIDEGROOM: No. Just a moment ago I felt the galloping.

FIRST YOUTH: It could have been another horse.

BRIDEGROOM [*intensely*]: Listen to me. There's only one horse in the whole world, and this one's it. Can't you understand that? If you're going to follow me, follow me without talking.

FIRST YOUTH: It's only that I want to . . .

BRIDEGROOM: Be quiet. I'm sure of meeting them there. Do you see this arm? Well, it's not my arm. It's my brother's arm, and my father's, and that of all the dead ones in my family. And it has so much strength that it can pull this tree up by the roots, if it wants to. And let's move on, because here I feel the clenched teeth of all my people in me so that I can't breathe easily.

BEGGAR WOMAN [*whining*]: Ay-y-y!

FIRST YOUTH: Did you hear that?

BRIDEGROOM: You go that way and then circle back.

FIRST YOUTH: This is a hunt.

BRIDEGROOM: A hunt. The greatest hunt there is.

[*The* YOUTH *goes off. The* BRIDEGROOM *goes rapidly to the left and stumbles over the* BEGGAR WOMAN, *Death.*]

BEGGAR WOMAN: Ay-y-y!

BRIDEGROOM: What do you want?

BEGGAR WOMAN: I'm cold.

BRIDEGROOM: Which way are you going?

BEGGAR WOMAN [*always whining like a beggar*]: Over there, far away . . .

BRIDEGROOM: Where are you from?

BEGGAR WOMAN: Over there . . . very far away.

BRIDEGROOM: Have you seen a man and a woman running away on a horse?

BEGGAR WOMAN [*awakening*]: Wait a minute . . .

[*She looks at him.*]

Handsome young man.

[*She rises.*]

But you'd be much handsomer sleeping.

BRIDEGROOM: Tell me; answer me. Did you see them?

BEGGAR WOMAN: Wait a minute . . . What broad shoulders! How would you like to be laid out on them and not have to walk on the soles of your feet which are so small?

BRIDEGROOM [*shaking her*]: I asked you if you saw them! Have they passed through here?

BEGGAR WOMAN [*energetically*]: No. They haven't passed; but they're coming from the hill. Don't you hear them?

BRIDEGROOM: No.

BEGGAR WOMAN: Do you know the road?

BRIDEGROOM: I'll go, whatever it's like!

BEGGAR WOMAN: I'll go along with you. I know this country.

BRIDEGROOM [*impatiently*]: Well, let's go! Which way?

BEGGAR WOMAN [*dramatically*]: This way!

[*They go rapidly out. Two violins, which represent the forest, are heard distantly. The* WOODCUTTERS *return. They have their axes on their shoulders. They move slowly among the tree trunks.*]

FIRST WOODCUTTER:

O rising death!
Death among the great leaves.

SECOND WOODCUTTER:

Don't open the gush of blood!

FIRST WOODCUTTER:

O lonely death!
Death among the dried leaves.

THIRD WOODCUTTER:

Don't lay flowers over the wedding!

SECOND WOODCUTTER:

O sad death!
Leave for their love a green branch.

FIRST WOODCUTTER:

O evil death!
Leave for their love a branch of green!

[*They go out while they are talking.* LEONARDO *and the* BRIDE *appear.*]

LEONARDO:

Hush!

BRIDE:

From here I'll go on alone.
You go now! I want you to turn back.

LEONARDO:

Hush, I said!

BRIDE:

With your teeth, with your hands, anyway you can,
take from my clean throat
the metal of this chain,
and let me live forgotten
back there in my house in the ground.
And if you don't want to kill me
as you would kill a tiny snake,
set in my hands, a bride's hands,
the barrel of your shotgun.
Oh, what lamenting, what fire,
sweeps upward through my head!
What glass splinters are stuck in my tongue!

LEONARDO:

We've taken the step now; hush!
because they're close behind us,
and I must take you with me.

BRIDE:

Then it must be by force!

LEONARDO:

By force? Who was it first
went down the stairway?

BRIDE:

I went down it.

LEONARDO:

And who was it put
a new bridle on the horse?

BRIDE:

I myself did it. It's true.

LEONARDO:

And whose were the hands
strapped spurs to my boots?

BRIDE:

> The same hands, these that are yours,
> but which when they see you would like
> to break the blue branches
> and sunder the purl of your veins.
> I love you! I love you! But leave me!
> For if I were able to kill you
> I'd wrap you round in a shroud
> with the edges bordered in violets.
> Oh, what lamenting, what fire,
> sweeps upward through my head!

LEONARDO:

> What glass splinters are stuck in my tongue!
> Because I tried to forget you
> and put a wall of stone
> between your house and mine.
> It's true. You remember?
> And when I saw you in the distance
> I threw sand in my eyes.
> But I was riding a horse
> and the horse went straight to your door.
> And the silver pins of your wedding
> turned my red blood black.
> And in me our dream was choking
> my flesh with its poisoned weeds.
> Oh, it isn't my fault –
> the fault is the earth's –
> and this fragrance that you exhale
> from your breasts and your braids.

BRIDE:

> Oh, how untrue! I want
> from you neither bed nor food,
> yet there's not a minute each day
> that I don't want to be with you,
> because you drag me, and I come,

then you tell me to go back
and I follow you,
like chaff blown on the breeze.
I have left a good, honest man,
and all his people,
with the wedding feast half-over
and wearing my bridal wreath.
But you are the one will be punished
and that I don't want to happen.
Leave me alone now! You run away!
There is no one who will defend you.

LEONARDO:

The birds of early morning
are calling among the trees.
The night is dying
on the stone's ridge.
Let's go to a hidden corner
where I may love you for ever,
for to me the people don't matter,
nor the venom they throw on us.

[*He embraces her strongly.*]

BRIDE:

And I'll sleep at your feet,
to watch over your dreams.
Naked, looking over the fields,
as though I were a bitch.
Because that's what I am! Oh, I look at you
and your beauty sears me.

LEONARDO:

Fire is stirred by fire.
The same tiny flame
will kill two wheat heads together.
Let's go!

BRIDE:

Where are you taking me?

LEONARDO:

> Where they cannot come,
> these men who surround us.
> Where I can look at you!

BRIDE [*sarcastically*]:

> Carry me with you from fair to fair,
> a shame to clean women,
> so that people will see me
> with my wedding sheets
> on the breeze like banners.

LEONARDO:

> I, too, would want to leave you
> if I thought as men should.
> But wherever you go, I go.
> You're the same. Take a step. Try.
> Nails of moonlight have fused
> my waist and your chains.

[*This whole scene is violent, full of great sensuality.*]

BRIDE:

> Listen!

LEONARDO:

> They're coming.

BRIDE:

> Run!
> It's fitting that I should die here,
> with water over my feet,
> with thorns upon my head.
> And fitting the leaves should mourn me,
> a woman lost and virgin.

LEONARDO:

> Be quiet. Now they're appearing.

BRIDE:

> Go now!

LEONARDO:

> Quiet. Don't let them hear us.

[*The* BRIDE *hesitates.*]

BRIDE:

Both of us!

LEONARDO [*embracing her*]:

Any way you want!
If they separate us, it will be
because I am dead.

BRIDE:

And I dead too.

[*They go out in each other's arms.*
The MOON *appears very slowly. The stage takes on a strong blue*
light. The two violins are heard. Suddenly two long, ear-splitting
shrieks are heard, and the music of the two violins is cut short. At the
second shriek the BEGGAR WOMAN *appears and stands with her back*
to the audience. She opens her cape and stands in the centre of the stage
like a great bird with immense wings. The MOON *halts. The curtain*
comes down in absolute silence.]

CURTAIN

ACT THREE

SCENE 2

The Final Scene

A white dwelling with arches and thick walls. To the right and left are white stairs. At the back, a great arch and a wall of the same colour. The floor also should be shining white. This simple dwelling should have the monumental feeling of a church. There should not be a single grey or any shadow, not even what is necessary for perspective.

[TWO GIRLS *dressed in dark blue are winding a red skein.*]

FIRST GIRL:

>Wool, red wool,
>what would you make?

SECOND GIRL:

>Oh, jasmine for dresses,
>fine wool like glass.
>At four o'clock born,
>at ten o'clock dead.
>A thread from this wool yarn,
>a chain round your feet
>a knot that will tighten
>the bitter white wreath.

LITTLE GIRL [*singing*]:

>Were you at the wedding?

FIRST GIRL:

>No.

LITTLE GIRL:

>Well, neither was I!
>What could have happened
>'midst the shoots of the vineyards?
>What could have happened

'neath the branch of the olive?
What really happened
that no one came back?
Were you at the wedding?

SECOND GIRL:

We told you once, no.

LITTLE GIRL [*leaving*]:

Well, neither was I!

SECOND GIRL:

Wool, red wool,
what would you sing?

FIRST GIRL:

Their wounds turning waxen,
balm-myrtle for pain.
Asleep in the morning,
and watching at night.

LITTLE GIRL [*in the doorway*]:

And then, the thread stumbled
on the flinty stones,
but mountains, blue mountains,
are letting it pass.
Running, running, running,
and finally to come
to stick in a knife blade,
to take back the bread.

[*She goes out.*]

SECOND GIRL:

Wool, red wool,
what would you tell?

FIRST GIRL:

The love is silent,
crimson the groom,
at the still shoreline
I saw them laid out.

[*She stops and looks at the skein.*]

LITTLE GIRL [*appearing in the doorway*]:

> Running, running, running,
> the thread runs to here.
> All covered with clay
> I feel them draw near.
> Bodies stretched stiffly
> in ivory sheets!

[*The* WIFE *and* MOTHER-IN-LAW *of* LEONARDO *appear. They are anguished.*]

FIRST GIRL: Are they coming yet?

MOTHER-IN-LAW [*harshly*]: We don't know.

SECOND GIRL: What can you tell us about the wedding?

FIRST GIRL: Yes, tell me.

MOTHER-IN-LAW [*curtly*]: Nothing.

LEONARDO'S WIFE: I want to go back and find out all about it.

MOTHER-IN-LAW [*sternly*]:

> You, back to your house.
> Brave and alone in your house.
> To grow old and to weep.
> But behind closed doors.
> Never again. Neither dead nor alive.
> We'll nail up our windows
> and let rains and nights
> fall on the bitter weeds.

LEONARDO'S WIFE: What could have happened?

MOTHER-IN-LAW:

> It doesn't matter what.
> Put a veil over your face.
> Your children are yours,
> that's all. On the bed
> put a cross of ashes
> where his pillow was.

[*They go out.*]

BEGGAR WOMAN [*at the door*]: A crust of bread, little girls.

LITTLE GIRL: Go away!

[*The* GIRLS *huddle close together.*]

BEGGAR WOMAN: Why?

LITTLE GIRL: Because you whine; go away!

FIRST GIRL: Child!

BEGGAR WOMAN:

> I might have asked for your eyes! A cloud
> of birds is following me. Will you have one?

LITTLE GIRL: I want to get away from here!

SECOND GIRL [*to the* BEGGAR WOMAN]: Don't mind her!

FIRST GIRL: Did you come by the road through the arroyo?

BEGGAR WOMAN: I came that way!

FIRST GIRL [*timidly*]: Can I ask you something?

BEGGAR WOMAN:

> I saw them: they'll be here soon: two torrents
> still at last, among the great boulders,
> two men at the horse's feet.
> Two dead men in the night's splendour.

[*With pleasure*]

> Dead, yes, dead.

FIRST GIRL: Hush, old woman, hush!

BEGGAR WOMAN:

> Crushed flowers for eyes, and their teeth
> two fistfuls of hard-frozen snow.
> Both of them fell, and the bride returns
> with bloodstains on her skirt and hair.
> And they come covered with two sheets
> carried on the shoulders of two tall boys.
> That's how it was; nothing more. What was
>   fitting.
> Over the golden flower, dirty sand.

[*She goes. The* GIRLS *bow their heads and start going out rhythmically.*]

FIRST GIRL:

> Dirty sand.

SECOND GIRL:

> Over the golden flower.

90

LITTLE GIRL:

> Over the golden flower
> they're bringing the dead from the arroyo.
> Dark the one,
> dark the other.
> What shadowy nightingale flies and weeps
> over the golden flower!

[She goes. The stage is left empty. The MOTHER *and a* NEIGHBOUR
WOMAN *appear. The* NEIGHBOUR *is weeping.]*

MOTHER: Hush.

NEIGHBOUR: I can't.

MOTHER: Hush, I said.

> *[At the door]*

Is there nobody here?

> *[She puts her hands to her forehead.]*

My son ought to answer me. But now my son is an armful of
shrivelled flowers. My son is a fading voice beyond the mountains
now.

> *[With rage, to the* NEIGHBOUR*]*

Will you shut up? I want no wailing in this house. Your tears are
only from your eyes, but when I'm alone mine will come – from
the soles of my feet, from my roots – burning more than blood.

NEIGHBOUR: You come to my house; don't you stay here.

MOTHER: I want to be here. Here. In peace. They're all dead now:
and at midnight I'll sleep, sleep without terror of guns or knives.
Other mothers will go to their windows, lashed by rain, to watch
for their sons' faces. But not I. And of my dreams I'll make a cold
ivory dove that will carry camellias of white frost to the graveyard. But no; not graveyard, not graveyard: the couch of earth,
the bed that shelters them and rocks them in the sky.

> *[A* WOMAN *dressed in black enters, goes toward the right, and there
> kneels. To the* NEIGHBOUR*]*

Take your hands from your face. We have terrible days ahead.
I want to see no one. The earth and I. My grief and I. And these
four walls. Ay-y-y! Ay-y-y!

[*She sits down, overcome.*]

NEIGHBOUR: Take pity on yourself!

MOTHER [*pushing back her hair*]: I must be calm.

[*She sits down.*]

Because the neighbour women will come and I don't want them to see me so poor. So poor! A woman without even one son to hold to her lips.

[*The* BRIDE *appears. She is without her wreath and wears a black shawl.*]

NEIGHBOUR [*with rage, seeing the* BRIDE]: Where are you going?

BRIDE: I'm coming here.

MOTHER [*to the* NEIGHBOUR]: Who is it?

NEIGHBOUR: Don't you recognize her?

MOTHER: That's why I asked who it was. Because I don't want to recognize her, so I won't sink my teeth in her throat. You snake!

[*She moves wrathfully on the* BRIDE, *then stops. To the* NEIGHBOUR]

Look at her! There she is, and she's crying, while I stand here calmly and don't tear her eyes out. I don't understand myself. Can it be I didn't love my son? But, where's his good name? Where is it now? Where is it?

[*She beats the* BRIDE *who drops to the floor.*]

NEIGHBOUR: For God's sake!

[*She tries to separate them.*]

BRIDE [*to the* NEIGHBOUR]: Let her; I came here so she'd kill me and they'd take me away with them.

[*To the* MOTHER]

But not with her hands; with grappling hooks, with a sickle – and with force – until they break on my bones. Let her! I want her to know I'm clean, that I may be crazy, but that they can bury me without a single man ever having seen himself in the whiteness of my breasts.

MOTHER: Shut up, shut up; what do I care about that?

BRIDE: Because I ran away with the other one; I ran away!

[*With anguish*]

You would have gone, too. I was a woman burning with desire, full of sores inside and out, and your son was a little bit of water from which I hoped for children, land, health; but the other one was a dark river, choked with brush, that brought near me the undertone of its rushes and its whispered song. And I went along with your son who was like a little boy of cold water – and the other sent against me hundreds of birds who got in my way and left white frost on my wounds, my wounds of a poor withered woman, of a girl caressed by fire. I didn't want to; remember that! I didn't want to. Your son was my destiny and I have not betrayed him, but the other one's arm dragged me along like the pull of the sea, like the head toss of a mule, and he would have dragged me always, always, always – even if I were an old woman and all your son's sons held me by the hair!

[*A* NEIGHBOUR *enters.*]

MOTHER: She is not to blame; nor am I!

[*Sarcastically*]

Who is, then? It's a delicate, lazy, sleepless woman who throws away an orange-blossom wreath and goes looking for a piece of bed warmed by another woman!

BRIDE: Be still! Be still! Take your revenge on me; here I am! See how soft my throat is; it would be less work for you than cutting a dahlia in your garden. But never that! Clean, clean as a new-born little girl. And strong enough to prove it to you. Light the fire. Let's stick our hands in; you, for your son, I, for my body. *You'll* draw yours out first.

[ANOTHER NEIGHBOUR *enters.*]

MOTHER: But what does your good name matter to me? What does your death matter to me? What does anything about anything matter to me? Blesséd be the wheat stalks, because my sons are under them: blesséd be the rain, because it wets the face of the dead. Blesséd be God, who stretches us out together to rest.

[ANOTHER NEIGHBOUR *enters.*]

BRIDE: Let me weep with you.

MOTHER: Weep. But at the door.

[*The* GIRL *enters. The* BRIDE *stays at the door. The* MOTHER *is at the centre of the stage.*]

LEONARDO'S WIFE [*entering and going to the left*]:

He was a beautiful horseman,
now he's a heap of snow.
He rode to fairs and mountains
and women's arms.
Now, the night's dark moss
crowns his forehead.

MOTHER:

A sunflower to your mother,
a mirror of the earth.
Let them put on your breast
the cross of bitter rosebay;
and over you a sheet
of shining silk;
between your quiet hands
let water form its lament.

WIFE:

Ay-y-y, four gallant boys
come with tired shoulders!

BRIDE:

Ay-y -y, four gallant boys
carry death on high!

MOTHER:

Neighbours.

LITTLE GIRL [*at the door*]:

They're bringing them now.

MOTHER:

It's the same thing.
Always the cross, the cross.

WOMEN:

Sweet nails,
cross adored,

sweet name
of Christ our Lord.

BRIDE: May the cross protect both the quick and the dead.

MOTHER:

Neighbours: with a knife,
with a little knife,
on their appointed day, between two and three,
these two men killed each other for love.
With a knife,
with a tiny knife
that barely fits the hand,
but that slides in clean
through the astonished flesh
and stops at the place
where trembles, enmeshed,
the dark root of a scream.

BRIDE:

And this is a knife,
a tiny knife
that barely fits the hand;
fish without scales, without river,
so that on their appointed day, between two and three,
with this knife,
two men are left stiff,
with their lips turning yellow.

MOTHER:

And it barely fits the hand
but it slides in clean
through the astonished flesh
and stops there, at the place
where trembles enmeshed
the dark root of a scream.

[*The* NEIGHBOURS, *kneeling on the floor, sob.*]

CURTAIN

YERMA

*A Tragic Poem in Three Acts
and Six Scenes*

Characters

—

Yerma
María
Juan
Victor
Pagan Crone
Dolores
First Laundress
Second Laundress
Third Laundress
Fourth Laundress
Fifth Laundress
Sixth Laundress
First Young Girl
Second Young Girl
The Female Mask
The Male Mask
First Sister-in-law
Second Sister-in-law
First Woman
Second Woman
The Child
First Man
Second Man
Third Man

ACT ONE

SCENE I

When the curtain rises YERMA *is asleep with an embroidery frame at her feet. The stage is in the strange light of a dream.*

> [*A* SHEPHERD *enters on tiptoe looking fixedly at* YERMA. *He leads by the hand a* CHILD *dressed in white. The clock sounds. When the* SHEPHERD *leaves, the light changes into the happy brightness of a spring morning.* YERMA *awakes.*]

VOICE [*within, singing*]:
>> For the nursey, nursey, nursey,
>> For the little nurse we'll make
>> A tiny hut out in the fields
>> And there we'll shelter take.

YERMA: Juan, do you hear me? Juan!

JUAN: Coming.

YERMA: It's time now.

JUAN: Did the oxen go by?

YERMA: They've already gone.

JUAN: See you later.

> [*He starts to leave.*]

YERMA: Won't you have a glass of milk?

JUAN: What for?

YERMA: You work a lot and your body's not strong enough for it.

JUAN: When men grow thin they get strong as steel.

YERMA: But not you. You were different when we were first married. Now you've got a face as white as though the sun had never shone on it. I'd like to see you go to the river and swim or climb up on the roof when the rain beats down on our house. Twenty-four months we've been married and you only get sadder, thinner, as if you were growing backwards.

JUAN: Are you finished?

YERMA [*rising*]: Don't take it wrong. If I were sick I'd like you to take care of me. 'My wife's sick. I'm going to butcher this lamb and cook her a good meat dish.' 'My wife's sick. I'm going to save this chicken-fat to relieve her chest; I'm going to take her this sheepskin to protect her feet from the snow.' That's the way I am. That's why I take care of you.

JUAN: I'm grateful.

YERMA: But you don't let me take care of you.

JUAN: Because there's nothing wrong with me. All these things are just your imagination. I work hard. Each year I'll get older.

YERMA: Each year. You and I will just go on here each year ...

JUAN [*smiling*]: Why, of course. And very peacefully. Our work goes well, we've no children to worry about.

YERMA: We've no children ... Juan!

JUAN: What is it?

YERMA: I love you, don't I?

JUAN: Yes, you love me.

YERMA: I know girls who trembled and cried before getting into bed with their husbands. Did I cry the first time I went to bed with you? Didn't I sing as I turned back the fine linen bedclothes? And didn't I tell you, 'These bedclothes smell of apples!'

JUAN: That's what you said!

YERMA: My mother cried because I wasn't sorry to leave her. And that's true! No one ever got married with more happiness. And yet ...

JUAN: Hush! I have a hard enough job hearing all the time that I'm ...

YERMA: No. Don't tell me what they say. I can see with my own eyes that that isn't so. The rain just by the force of its falling on the stones softens them and makes weeds grow – weeds which people say aren't good for anything. 'Weeds aren't good for anything', yet I see them plainly enough – moving their yellow flowers in the wind.

JUAN: We've got to wait!

YERMA: Yes; loving each other.

[YERMA *embraces and kisses her husband. She takes the initiative.*]

JUAN: If you need anything, tell me, and I'll bring it to you. You
know well enough I don't like you to be going out.

YERMA: I never go out.

JUAN: You're better off here.

YERMA: Yes.

JUAN: The street's for people with nothing to do.

YERMA [*darkly*]: Of course.

[JUAN *leaves.* YERMA *walks toward her sewing. She passes a hand
over her belly, lifts her arms in a beautiful sigh, and sits down to sew.*]

YERMA:

> From where do you come, my love, my baby?
> 'From the mountains of icy cold.'
> What do you lack, sweet love, my baby?
> 'The woven warmth in your dress.'

[*She threads the needle.*]

> Let the branches tremble in the sun
> and the fountains leap all around!

[*As if she spoke to a child*]

> In the courtyard the dog barks,
> In the trees the wind sings.
> The oxen low for the ox-herd,
> and the moon curls up my hair.
> What want you, boy, from so far away?

[*Pause.*]

> 'The mountains white upon your chest.'
> Let the branches tremble in the sun
> and the fountains leap all around!

[*Sewing*]

> I shall say to you, child, yes,
> for you I'll torn and broken be.
> How painful is this belly now,
> where first you shall be cradled!
> When, boy, when will you come to me?

[*Pause.*]

'When sweet your flesh of jasmine smells.'
Let the branches tremble in the sun
and the fountains leap all around!

[YERMA *continues singing.* MARÍA *enters through the door carrying a bundle of clothes.*]

YERMA: Where are you coming from?

MARÍA: From the store.

YERMA: From the store so early?

MARÍA: For what I wanted, I'd have waited at the door till they opened. Can't you guess what I bought?

YERMA: You probably bought some coffee for breakfast; sugar, bread.

MARÍA: No. I bought laces, three lengths of linen, ribbons, and coloured wool to make tassels. My husband had the money and he gave it to me without my even asking for it.

YERMA: You're going to make a blouse?

MARÍA: No, it's because . . . Can't you guess?

YERMA: What?

MARÍA: Because . . . well . . . it's here now!

[*She lowers her head.* YERMA *rises and looks at her in admiration.*]

YERMA: In just five months!

MARÍA: Yes.

YERMA: You can tell it's there?

MARÍA: Naturally.

YERMA [*with curiosity*]: But, how does it make you feel?

MARÍA: I don't know. Sad; upset.

YERMA: Sad? Upset?

[*Holding her.*]

But . . . when did he come? Tell me about it. You weren't expecting him.

MARÍA: No, I wasn't expecting him.

YERMA: Why, you might have been singing; yes? I sing. You . . . tell me . . .

MARÍA: Don't ask me about it. Have you ever held a live bird pressed in your hand?

YERMA: Yes.

MARÍA: Well – the same way – but more in your blood.

YERMA: How beautiful!

[*She looks at her, beside herself.*]

MARÍA: I'm confused. I don't know anything.

YERMA: About what?

MARÍA: About what I must do. I'll ask my mother.

YERMA: What for? She's old now and she'll have forgotten about these things. Don't walk very much, and when you breathe, breathe as softly as if you had a rose between your teeth.

MARÍA: You know, they say that later he kicks you gently with his little legs.

YERMA: And that's when you love him best, when you can really say: '*My* child!'

MARÍA: In the midst of all this, I feel ashamed.

YERMA: What has your husband said about it?

MARÍA: Nothing.

YERMA: Does he love you a lot?

MARÍA: He doesn't tell me so, but when he's close to me his eyes tremble like two green leaves.

YERMA: Did he know that you were . . . ?

MARÍA: Yes.

YERMA: But, how did he know it?

MARÍA: I don't know. But on our wedding night he kept telling me about it with his mouth pressed against my cheek; so that now it seems to me my child is a dove of fire he made slip in through my ear.

YERMA: Oh, how lucky you are!

MARÍA: But you know more about these things than I do.

YERMA: And what good does it do me?

MARÍA: That's true! Why should it be like that? Out of all the brides of your time you're the only one who . . .

YERMA: That's the way it is. Of course, there's still time. Helena was three years, and long ago some in my mother's time were much longer, but two years and twenty days – like me – is too long to wait. I don't think it's right for me to burn myself out here. Many nights I go barefooted to the patio to walk on the ground. I don't know why I do it. If I keep on like this, I'll end by turning bad.

MARÍA: But look here, you infant, you're talking as if you were an old woman. You listen to me, now! No one can complain about these things. A sister of my mother's had one after fourteen years, and you should have seen what a beautiful child that was!

YERMA [*eagerly*]: What was he like?

MARÍA: He used to bellow like a little bull, as loud as a thousand locusts all buzzing at once, and wet us, and pull our braids; and when he was four months old he scratched our faces all over.

YERMA [*laughing*]: But those things don't hurt.

MARÍA: Let me tell you –

YERMA: Bah! I've seen my sister nurse her child with her breasts full of scratches. It gave her great pain, but it was a fresh pain – good, and necessary for health.

MARÍA: They say one suffers a lot with children.

YERMA: That's a lie. That's what weak, complaining mothers say. What do they have them for? Having a child is no bouquet of roses. We must suffer to see them grow. I sometimes think half our blood must go. But that's good, healthy, beautiful. Every woman has blood for four or five children, and when she doesn't have them it turns to poison . . . as it will in me.

MARÍA: I don't know what's the matter with me.

YERMA: I've always heard it said that you're frightened the first time.

MARÍA [*timidly*]: We'll see. You know, you sew so well that . . .

YERMA [*taking the bundle*]: Give it here. I'll cut you two little dresses. And this . . . ?

MARÍA: For diapers.

YERMA [*she sits down*]: All right.

MARÍA: Well . . . See you later.

[*As she comes near,* YERMA *lovingly presses her hands against her belly.*]

YERMA: Don't run on the cobblestones.

MARÍA: Good-bye.

[*She kisses her and leaves.*]

YERMA: Come back soon.

[YERMA *is in the same attitude as at the beginning of the scene. She takes her scissors and starts to cut.* VICTOR *enters.*]

Hello, Victor.

VICTOR [*he is deep-looking and has a firm gravity about him*]: Where's Juan?

YERMA: Out in the fields.

VICTOR: What's that you're sewing?

YERMA: I'm cutting some diapers.

VICTOR [*smiling*]: Well, now!

YERMA [*laughs*]: I'm going to border them with lace.

VICTOR: If it's a girl, you give her your name.

YERMA [*trembling*]: How's that?

VICTOR: I'm happy for you.

YERMA [*almost choking*]: No ... they aren't for me. They're for María's child.

VICTOR: Well then, let's see if her example will encourage you. This house needs a child in it.

YERMA [*with anguish*]: Needs one!

VICTOR: Well, get along with it. Tell your husband to think less about his work. He wants to make money and he will, but who's he going to leave it to when he dies? I'm going out with my sheep. Tell Juan to take out the two he bought from me, and about this other thing – try harder!

[*He leaves, smiling.*]

YERMA [*passionately*]: That's it! Try ... !

> I shall say to you, child, yes,
> for you I'll torn and broken be.
> How painful is this belly now,
> where first you shall be cradled!
> When, child, when will you come to me?

[YERMA, *who has risen thoughtfully, goes to the place where* VICTOR *stood, and breathes deeply – like one who breathes mountain air. Then she goes to the other side of the room as if looking for something, and after that sits down and takes up the sewing again. She begins to sew. Her eyes remain fixed on one point.*

CURTAIN

ACT ONE

SCENE 2

[*A field.* YERMA *enters carrying a basket. The* FIRST OLD WOMAN *enters.*]

YERMA: Good morning!

FIRST OLD WOMAN: Good morning to a beautiful girl! Where are you going?

YERMA: I've just come from taking dinner to my husband who's working in the olive groves.

FIRST OLD WOMAN: Have you been married very long?

YERMA: Three years.

FIRST OLD WOMAN: Do you have any children?

YERMA: No.

FIRST OLD WOMAN: Bah! You'll have them!

YERMA [*eagerly*]: Do you think so?

FIRST OLD WOMAN: Well, why not?

[*She sits down.*]

I, too, have just taken my husband his food. He's old. He still has to work. I have nine children, like nine golden suns, but since not one of them is a girl, here you have me going from one side to the other.

YERMA: You live on the other side of the river?

FIRST OLD WOMAN: Yes. In the mills. What family are you from?

YERMA: I'm Enrique the shepherd's daughter.

FIRST OLD WOMAN: Ah! Enrique the shepherd. I knew him. Good people. Get up, sweat, eat some bread, and die. No playing, no nothing. The fairs for somebody else. Silent creatures. I could have married an uncle of yours, but then . . . ! I've been a woman with her skirts to the wind. I've run like an arrow to melon cuttings, to parties, to sugar cakes. Many times at dawn I've rushed to the door thinking I heard the music of guitars going along and coming nearer, but it was only the wind.

[*She laughs.*]

You'll laugh at me. I've had two husbands, fourteen children – five of them dead – and yet I'm not sad, and I'd like to live much longer. That's what I say! The fig trees, how they last! The houses, how they last! And only we poor bedevilled women turn to dust for any reason.

YERMA: I'd like to ask you a question.

FIRST OLD WOMAN: Let's see.

[*She looks at her.*]

I know what you're going to ask me, and there's not a word you can say about those things.

[*She rises.*]

YERMA [*holding her*]: But, why not? Hearing you talk has given me confidence. For some time I've been wanting to talk about it with an older woman – because I want to find out. Yes, you can tell me –

FIRST OLD WOMAN: Tell you what?

YERMA [*lowering her voice*]: What you already know. Why am I childless? Must I be left in the prime of my life taking care of little birds, or putting up tiny pleated curtains at my little windows? No. You've got to tell me what to do, for I'll do anything you tell me – even to sticking needles in the weakest part of my eyes.

FIRST OLD WOMAN: Me, tell you? I don't know anything about it. I laid down face up and began to sing. Children came like water. Oh, who can say this body we've got isn't beautiful? You take a step and at the end of the street a horse whinnies. Ay-y-y! Leave me alone, girl; don't make me talk. I have a lot of ideas I don't want to tell you about.

YERMA: Why not? I never talk about anything else with my husband!

FIRST OLD WOMAN: Listen. Does your husband please you?

YERMA: What?

FIRST OLD WOMAN: I mean – do you really love him? Do you long to be with him?

YERMA: I don't know.

FIRST OLD WOMAN: Don't you tremble when he comes near you? Don't you feel something like a dream when he brings his lips close to yours? Tell me.

YERMA: No. I've never noticed it.

FIRST OLD WOMAN: Never? Not even when you've danced?

YERMA [remembering]: Perhaps . . . one time . . . with Victor . . .

FIRST OLD WOMAN: Go on.

YERMA: He took me by the waist and I couldn't say a word to him, because I couldn't talk. Another time this same Victor, when I was fourteen years old – he was a husky boy – took me in his arms to leap a ditch and I started shaking so hard my teeth chattered. But I've always been shy.

FIRST OLD WOMAN: But with your husband . . . ?

YERMA: My husband's something else. My father gave him to me and I took him. With happiness. That's the plain truth. Why, from the first day I was engaged to him I thought about . . . our children. And I could see myself in his eyes. Yes, but it was to see myself reflected very small, very manageable, as if I were my own daughter.

FIRST OLD WOMAN: It was just the opposite with me. Maybe that's why you haven't had a child yet. Men have got to give us pleasure, girl. They've got to take down our hair and let us drink water out of their mouths. So runs the world.

YERMA: Your world, but not mine. I think about a lot of things, a lot, and I'm sure that the things I think about will come true in my son. I gave myself over to my husband for his sake, and I go on giving to see if he'll be born – but never just for pleasure.

FIRST OLD WOMAN: And the only result is – you're empty!

YERMA: No, not empty, because I'm filling up with hate. Tell me; is it my fault? In a man do you have to look for only the man, nothing more? Then, what are you going to think when he lets you lie in bed looking at the ceiling with sad eyes, and he turns over and goes to sleep? Should I go on thinking of him or what can come shining out of my breast? I don't know; but you tell me – out of charity!

[*She kneels.*]

FIRST OLD WOMAN: Oh, what an open flower! What a beautiful creature you are. You leave me alone. Don't make me say any more. I don't want to talk with you any more. These are matters of honour. And I don't burn anyone's honour. You'll find out. But you certainly ought to be less innocent.

YERMA [*sadly*]: Girls like me who grow up in the country have all doors closed to them. Everything becomes half-words, gestures, because all these things, they say, must not be talked about. And you, too; you, too, stop talking and go off with the air of a doctor – knowing everything, but keeping it from one who dies of thirst.

FIRST OLD WOMAN: To any other calm woman, I could speak; not to you. I'm an old woman and I know what I'm saying.

YERMA: Then, God help me.

FIRST OLD WOMAN: Not God; I've never liked God. When will people realize he doesn't exist? Men are the ones who'll have to help you.

YERMA: But, why do you tell me that? Why?

FIRST OLD WOMAN [*leaving*]: Though there should be a God, even a tiny one, to send his lightning against those men of rotted seed who make puddles out of the happiness of the fields.

YERMA: I don't know what you're trying to tell me.

FIRST OLD WOMAN: Well, I know what I'm trying to say. Don't you be unhappy. Hope for the best. You're still very young. What do you want me to do?

[*She leaves.* TWO GIRLS *appear.*]

FIRST GIRL: Everywhere we go we meet people.

YERMA: With all the work, the men have to be in the olive groves, and we must take them their food. No one's left at home but the old people.

SECOND GIRL: Are you on your way back to the village?

YERMA: I'm going that way.

FIRST GIRL: I'm in a great hurry. I left my baby asleep and there's no one in the house.

YERMA: Then hurry up, woman. You can't leave babies alone like that. Are there any pigs at your place?

FIRST GIRL: No. But you're right. I'm going right away.

YERMA: Go on. That's how things happen. Surely you've locked him in?

FIRST GIRL: Naturally.

YERMA: Yes, but even so, we don't realize what a tiny child is. The thing that seems most harmless to us might finish him off. A little needle. A swallow of water.

FIRST GIRL: You're right. I'm on my way. I just don't think of those things.

YERMA: Get along now!

SECOND GIRL: If you had four or five, you wouldn't talk like that.

YERMA: Why not? Even if I had forty.

SECOND GIRL: Anyway, you and I, not having any, live more peacefully.

YERMA: Not I.

SECOND GIRL: I do. What a bother! My mother, on the other hand, does nothing but give me herbs so I'll have them, and in October we're going to the saint who, they say, gives them to women who ask for them eagerly. My mother will ask for them, not I.

YERMA: Then, why did you marry?

SECOND GIRL: Because they married me off. They get everyone married. If we keep on like this, the only unmarried ones will be the little girls. Well, anyway, you really get married long before you go to the church. But the old women keep worrying about all these things. I'm nineteen and I don't like to cook or do washing. Well, now I have to spend the whole day doing what I don't like to do. And all for what? We did the same things as sweethearts that we do now. It's all just the old folks' silly ideas.

YERMA: Be quiet; don't talk that way.

SECOND GIRL: You'll be calling me crazy, too. That crazy girl – that crazy girl!

[*She laughs.*]

I'll tell you the only thing I've learned from life: everybody's stuck inside their house doing what they don't like to do. How much better it is out in the streets. Sometimes I go to the arroyo, sometimes I climb up and ring the bells, or again I might just take a drink of anisette.

YERMA: You're only a child.

SECOND GIRL: Why, yes – but I'm not crazy.

[*She laughs.*]

YERMA: Doesn't your mother live at the topmost door in the village?

SECOND GIRL: Yes.

YERMA: In the last house?

SECOND GIRL: Yes.

YERMA: What's her name?

SECOND GIRL: Dolores. Why do you ask?

YERMA: Oh, nothing.

SECOND GIRL: You wouldn't be asking because of . . . ?

YERMA: I don't know . . . people say . . .

SECOND GIRL: Well, that's up to you. Look, I'm going to take my husband his food.

[*She laughs.*]

That's something to see! Too bad I can't say my sweetheart, isn't it?

[*She laughs.*]

Here comes that crazy girl!

[*She leaves, laughing happily.*]

Good-bye!

VICTOR'S VOICE [*singing*]:

     Why, shepherd, sleep alone?
     Why, shepherd, sleep alone?
     On my wool-quilt deep
     you'd finer sleep.
     Why, shepherd, sleep alone?

YERMA [*listening*]:

     Why, shepherd, sleep alone?

On my wool-quilt deep
you'd finer sleep.
Your quilt of shadowed stone,
    shepherd,
and your shirt of frost,
    shepherd,
grey rushes of the winter
on the night-tide of your bed.
The oak-roots weave their needles,
    shepherd,
Beneath your pillow silently,
    shepherd,
and if you hear a woman's voice
it's the torn voice of the stream.
    Shepherd, shepherd.
What does the hillside want of you,
    Shepherd?
Hillside of bitter weeds.
What child is killing you?
The thorn the broom-tree bore!

[*She starts to leave and meets* VICTOR *as he enters.*]

VICTOR [*happily*]: Where is all this beauty going?

YERMA: Was that you singing?

VICTOR: Yes.

YERMA: How well you sing! I'd never heard you.

VICTOR: No?

YERMA: And what a vibrant voice! It's like a stream of water that fills your mouth.

VICTOR: I'm always happy.

YERMA: That's true.

VICTOR: Just as you're sad.

YERMA: I'm not usually sad, but I have reason to be.

VICTOR: And your husband's sadder than you.

YERMA: He is, yes. It's his character – dry.

VICTOR: He was always like that.

[*Pause.* YERMA *is seated.*]

Did you take his supper to him?

YERMA: Yes.

[*She looks at him. Pause.*]

What have you here?

[*She points to his face.*]

VICTOR: Where?

YERMA [*she rises and stands near* VICTOR]: Here ... on your cheek. Like a burn.

VICTOR: It's nothing.

YERMA: It looked like one to me.

[*Pause.*]

VICTOR: It must be the sun ...

YERMA: Perhaps ...

[*Pause. The silence is accentuated and without the slightest gesture, a struggle between the two begins.*]

YERMA [*trembling*]: Do you hear that?

VICTOR: What?

YERMA: Don't you hear a crying?

VICTOR [*listening*]: No.

YERMA: I thought I heard a child crying.

VICTOR: Yes?

YERMA: Very near. And he cried as though drowning.

VICTOR: There are always a lot of children around here who come to steal fruit.

YERMA: No, it's the voice of a small child.

[*Pause.*]

VICTOR: I don't hear anything.

YERMA: I probably just imagined it.

[*She looks at him fixedly.* VICTOR *also looks at her, then slowly shifts his gaze as if afraid.* JUAN *enters.*]

JUAN: Still here? What are you doing here?

YERMA: I was talking.

VICTOR: Salud!

[*He leaves.*]

JUAN: You should be at home.

YERMA: I was delayed.

JUAN: I don't see what kept you.

YERMA: I heard the birds sing.

JUAN: That's all very well. But this is just the way to give people something to talk about.

YERMA [*strongly*]: Juan, what can you be thinking?

JUAN: I don't say it because of you. I say it because of other people.

YERMA: Other people be damned!

JUAN: Don't curse. That's ugly in a woman.

YERMA: I wish I were a woman.

JUAN: Let's stop talking. You go home.

    [*Pause.*]

YERMA: All right. Shall I expect you?

JUAN: No. I'll be busy all night with the irrigating. There's very little water; it's mine till sun-up, and I've got to guard it from thieves. You go to bed and sleep.

YERMA [*dramatically*]: I'll sleep.

    [*She leaves.*]

CURTAIN

ACT TWO

SCENE I

A fast-flowing mountain stream where the village women wash their clothes. The LAUNDRESSES *are arranged at various levels.*

[*Song before the curtain rises.*]

SONG

> Here in this icy current
> let me wash your lace,
> just like a glowing jasmine
> is your laughing face.

FIRST LAUNDRESS: I don't like to be talking.

SECOND LAUNDRESS: Well, we talk here.

FOURTH LAUNDRESS: And there's no harm in it.

FIFTH LAUNDRESS: Whoever wants a good name, let her earn it.

FOURTH LAUNDRESS:

> I planted thyme,
> I watched it grow.
> Who wants a good name
> Must live just so.

[*They laugh.*]

FIFTH LAUNDRESS: That's the way we talk.

FIRST LAUNDRESS: But we never really know anything for certain.

FOURTH LAUNDRESS: Well, it's certain enough that her husband's brought his two sisters to live with them.

FIFTH LAUNDRESS: The old maids?

FOURTH LAUNDRESS: Yes. They used to watch the church, and now they watch their sister-in-law. I wouldn't be able to live with them.

FIRST LAUNDRESS: Why not?

FOURTH LAUNDRESS: They'd give me the creeps. They're like those big leaves that quickly spring up over graves. They're smeared with wax. They grow inwards. I figure they must fry their food with lamp oil.

THIRD LAUNDRESS: And they're in the house now?

FOURTH LAUNDRESS: Since yesterday. Her husband's going back to his fields again now.

FIRST LAUNDRESS: But can't anyone find out what happened?

FIFTH LAUNDRESS: She spent the night before last sitting on her doorstep – in spite of the cold.

FIRST LAUNDRESS: But why?

FOURTH LAUNDRESS: It's hard work for her to stay in the house.

FIFTH LAUNDRESS: That's the way those mannish creatures are. When they could be making lace, or apple cakes, they like to climb up on the roof, or go wade barefoot in the river.

FIRST LAUNDRESS: Who are you to be talking like that? She hasn't any children but that's not her fault.

FOURTH LAUNDRESS: The one who wants children, has them. These spoiled, lazy, and soft girls aren't up to having a wrinkled belly.

[They laugh.]

THIRD LAUNDRESS: And they dash face powder and rouge on themselves, and pin on sprigs of oleander, and go looking for some man who's not their husband.

FIFTH LAUNDRESS: Nothing could be truer!

FIRST LAUNDRESS: But have you seen her with anybody?

FOURTH LAUNDRESS: We haven't, but other people have.

FIRST LAUNDRESS: Always other people!

FIFTH LAUNDRESS: On two separate occasions, they say.

SECOND LAUNDRESS: And what were they doing?

FOURTH LAUNDRESS: Talking.

FIRST LAUNDRESS: Talking's no sin.

FOURTH LAUNDRESS: In this world just a glance can be something. My mother always said that. A woman looking at roses isn't the same thing as a woman looking at a man's thighs. And she looks at him.

FIRST LAUNDRESS: But at whom?

FOURTH LAUNDRESS: Someone. Haven't you heard? You find out for yourself. Do you want me to say it louder?

[*Laughter.*]

And when she's not looking at him – when she's alone, when he's not right in front of her – she carries his picture – in her eyes.

FIRST LAUNDRESS: That's a lie!

[*There is excitement.*]

FIFTH LAUNDRESS: But what about her husband?

THIRD LAUNDRESS: Her husband acts like a deaf man. Just stands around blankly – like a lizard taking the sun.

[*Laughter.*]

FIRST LAUNDRESS: All this would take care of itself if they had children.

SECOND LAUNDRESS: All this comes of people not being content with their lot.

FOURTH LAUNDRESS: Every passing hour makes the hell in that house worse. She and her sisters-in-law, never opening their lips, scrub the walls all day, polish the copper, clean the windows with steam, and oil the floors: but the more the house shines, the more it seethes inside.

FIRST LAUNDRESS: It's all his fault; his. When a man doesn't give children, he's got to take care of his wife.

FOURTH LAUNDRESS: It's her fault – because she's got a tongue hard as flint.

FIRST LAUNDRESS: What devil's got into your hair that makes you talk that way?

FOURTH LAUNDRESS: Well! Who gave your tongue permission to give me advice?

SECOND LAUNDRESS: Quiet, you two!

FIRST LAUNDRESS: I'd like to string all these clacking tongues on a knitting-needle.

SECOND LAUNDRESS: Quiet, you!

FOURTH LAUNDRESS: And I the nipples of all hypocrites.

SECOND LAUNDRESS: Hush up! Can't you see? Here come the sisters-in-law.

ACT TWO

[*There is whispering. Yerma's* TWO SISTERS-IN-LAW *enter. They are dressed in mourning. In the silence, they start their washing. Sheep bells are heard.*]

FIRST LAUNDRESS: Are the shepherds leaving already?

THIRD LAUNDRESS: Yes, all the flocks leave today.

FOURTH LAUNDRESS [*taking a deep breath*]: I like the smell of sheep.

THIRD LAUNDRESS: You do?

FOURTH LAUNDRESS: Yes. And why not? The smell of what's ours. Just as I like the smell of the red mud this river carries in the winter.

THIRD LAUNDRESS: Whims!

FIFTH LAUNDRESS [*looking*]: All the flocks are leaving together.

FOURTH LAUNDRESS: It's a flood of wool. They sweep everything along. If the green wheat had eyes it'd tremble to see them coming.

THIRD LAUNDRESS: Look how they run! What a band of devils!

FIRST LAUNDRESS: They're all out now, not a flock is missing.

FOURTH LAUNDRESS: Let's see. No . . . Yes, yes. One is missing.

FIFTH LAUNDRESS: Which one?

FOURTH LAUNDRESS: Victor's.

[*The* TWO SISTERS-IN-LAW *sit up and look at each other.*]

FOURTH LAUNDRESS [*singing*]:

> Here in this icy current
> let me wash your lace.
> Just like a glowing jasmine
> is your laughing face.
> I would like to live
> within the tiny snowstorm
> that the jasmines give.

FIRST LAUNDRESS:

> Alas for the barren wife!
> Alas for her whose breasts are sand!

FIFTH LAUNDRESS:

> Tell me if your husband
> has fertile seed
> so water through your clothes
> will sing indeed.

FOURTH LAUNDRESS:

> Your petticoat to me
> is silvery boat and breeze
> that sweep along the sea.

FIRST LAUNDRESS:

> These clothes that are my baby's
> I wash here in the stream
> to teach the stream a lesson
> how crystal-like to gleam.

SECOND LAUNDRESS:

> Down the hillside he comes
> at lunchtime to me,
> my husband with one rose
> and I give him three.

FIFTH LAUNDRESS:

> Through meadows at dusk comes
> my husband to eat.
> To live coals he brings me
> I give myrtle sweet.

FOURTH LAUNDRESS:

> Through night skies he comes,
> my husband, to bed.
> I, like red gillyflowers,
> he, a gillyflower red.

FIRST LAUNDRESS:

> And flower to flower must be wed
> when summer dries the reaper's blood so red.

FOURTH LAUNDRESS:

> And wombs be opened to birds without sleep
> when winter tries the door and cold's to keep.

FIRST LAUNDRESS:

> The bedclothes must receive our tears.

FOURTH LAUNDRESS:

> But we must sing in bed!

FIFTH LAUNDRESS:

> When the husband comes
> to bring the wreath and bread.

FOURTH LAUNDRESS:

> Because our arms must intertwine.

SECOND LAUNDRESS:

> Because in our throats the light is rent.

FOURTH LAUNDRESS:

> Because the leaf-stem becomes fine.

FIRST LAUNDRESS:

> And the hill is covered with a breeze's tent.

SIXTH LAUNDRESS [*appearing at the topmost part of the swiftly flowing stream*]:

> So that a child may weld
> white crystals in the dawn.

FIRST LAUNDRESS:

> And in our waists be held
> torn stems of coral tree.

SIXTH LAUNDRESS:

> So that oarsmen there will be
> in the waters of the sea.

FIRST LAUNDRESS:

> A tiny child, one.

SECOND LAUNDRESS:

> And when the doves stretch wing and beak

THIRD LAUNDRESS:

> an infant weeps, a son.

FOURTH LAUNDRESS:

> And men push ever forward
> like stags by wounds made weak.

FIFTH LAUNDRESS:

> Joy, joy, joy!
> of the swollen womb beneath the dress!

SECOND LAUNDRESS:

Joy, joy, joy!
The waist can miracles possess!

FIRST LAUNDRESS:

But, alas for the barren wife!
Alas for her whose breasts are sand!

THIRD LAUNDRESS:

Let her shine out resplendent!

FOURTH LAUNDRESS:

Let her run!

FIFTH LAUNDRESS:

And shine out resplendent again!

FIRST LAUNDRESS:

Let her sing!

SECOND LAUNDRESS:

Let her hide!

FIRST LAUNDRESS:

And sing once more.

SECOND LAUNDRESS:

Of whiteness like the dawn's
my baby's clean clothes store.

FIRST AND SECOND LAUNDRESSES [*they sing together*]:

Here in this icy current
let me wash your lace.
Just like a glowing jasmine
is your laughing face.
Ha! Ha! Ha!

[*They move the clothes in rhythm and beat them.*]

CURTAIN

ACT TWO

SCENE 2

YERMA's *house. It is twilight.* JUAN *is seated. The* TWO SISTERS-IN-LAW *are standing.*

JUAN: You say she went out a little while ago?

[*The* OLDER SISTER *answers with a nod.*]

She's probably at the fountain. But you've known all along I don't like her to go out alone.

[*Pause.*]

You can set the table.

[*The* YOUNGER SISTER *enters.*]

The bread I eat is hard enough earned!

[*To his* SISTER]

I had a hard day yesterday. I was pruning the apple trees, and when evening fell I started to wonder why I should put so much into my work if I can't even lift an apple to my mouth. I'm tired.

[*He passes his hand over his face. Pause.*]

That woman's still not here. One of you should go out with her. That's why you're here eating at my table and drinking my wine. My life's in the fields, but my honour's here. And my honour is yours too.

[*The* SISTER *bows her head.*]

Don't take that wrong.

[YERMA *enters carrying two pitchers. She stands at the door.*]

Have you been to the fountain?

YERMA: So we'd have fresh water for supper.

How are the fields?

JUAN: Yesterday I pruned the trees.

[YERMA *sets the pitchers down. Pause.*]

YERMA: Are you going to stay in?

JUAN: I have to watch the flocks. You know that's an owner's duty.

YERMA: I know it very well. Don't repeat it.

JUAN: Each man has his life to lead.

YERMA: And each woman hers. I'm not asking you to stay. I have everything I need here. Your sisters guard me well. Soft bread and cheese and roast lamb I eat here, and in the field your cattle eat grass softened with dew. I think you can live in peace.

JUAN: In order to live in peace, one must be contented.

YERMA: And you're not?

JUAN: No. I'm not.

YERMA: Don't say what you started to.

JUAN: Don't you know my way of thinking? The sheep in the fold and women at home. You go out too much. Haven't you always heard me say that?

YERMA: Justly. Women in their homes. When those homes aren't tombs. When the chairs break and the linen sheets wear out with use. But not here. Each night, when I go to bed, I find my bed newer, more shining – as if it had just been brought from the city.

JUAN: You yourself realize that I've a right to complain. That I have reasons to be on the alert!

YERMA: Alert? For what? I don't offend you in any way. I live obedient to you, and what I suffer I keep close in my flesh. And every day that passes will be worse. Let's be quiet now. I'll learn to bear my cross as best I can, but don't ask me for anything. If I could suddenly turn into an old woman and have a mouth like a withered flower, I could smile and share my life with you. But now – now you leave me alone with my thorns.

JUAN: You speak in a way I don't understand. I don't deprive you of anything. I send to nearby towns for the things you like. I have my faults, but I want peace and quiet with you. I want to be sleeping out in the fields – thinking that you're sleeping too.

YERMA: But I don't sleep. I can't sleep.

JUAN: Is it because you need something? Tell me. Answer me!

YERMA [*deliberately, looking fixedly at her husband*]: Yes, I need something.

[*Pause.*]

JUAN: Always the same thing. It's more than five years. I've almost forgotten about it.

YERMA: But I'm not you. Men get other things out of life: their cattle, trees, conversations, but women have only their children and the care of their children.

JUAN: Everybody's not the same way. Why don't you bring one of your brother's children here? I don't oppose that.

YERMA: I don't want to take care of somebody else's children. I think my arms would freeze from holding them.

JUAN: You brood on this one idea till you're half-crazy – instead of thinking about something else – and you persist in running your head against a stone.

YERMA: A stone, yes; and it's shameful that it is a stone, because it ought to be a basket of flowers and sweet scents.

JUAN: At your side one feels nothing but uneasiness, dissatisfaction. As a last resort, you should resign yourself.

YERMA: I didn't come to these four walls to resign myself. When a cloth binds my head so my mouth won't drop open, and my hands are tied tight in my coffin – then, then I'll resign myself!

JUAN: Well then, what do you want to do?

YERMA: I want to drink water and there's neither water nor a glass. I want to go up the mountain, and I have no feet. I want to embroider skirts and I can't find thread.

JUAN: What's happened is that you're not a real woman, and you're trying to ruin a man who has no choice in the matter.

YERMA: I don't know what I am. Let me walk around; get myself in hand again. I have in no way failed you.

JUAN: I don't like people to be pointing me out. That's why I want to see this door closed and each person in his house.

[*The* FIRST SISTER *enters slowly and walks toward some shelves.*]

YERMA: It's no sin to talk with people.

JUAN: But it can seem one.

[*The other* SISTER *enters and goes toward the water jars, from one of which she fills a pitcher.*]

125

JUAN [*lowering his voice*]: I'm not strong enough for this sort of thing. When people talk to you, shut your mouth and remember you're a married woman.

YERMA [*with surprise*]: Married!

JUAN: And that families have honour. And that honour is a burden that rests on all.

[*The* SISTER *leaves slowly with the pitcher.*]

But that it's both dark and weak in the same channels of the blood.

[*The other* SISTER *leaves with a platter in almost a processional manner. Pause.*]

Forgive me.

[YERMA *looks at her husband. He raises his head and his glance catches her.*]

Even though you look at me so that I oughtn't to say to you: 'Forgive me', but force you to obey me, lock you up, because that's what I'm the husband for.

[*The* TWO SISTERS *appear at the door.*]

YERMA: I beg you not to talk about it. Let the matter rest.

JUAN: Let's go eat.

[*The* TWO SISTERS *leave.*]

Did you hear me?

YERMA [*sweetly*]: You eat with your sisters. I'm not hungry yet.

JUAN: As you wish.

[*He leaves.*]

YERMA [*as though dreaming*]:

Oh, what a field of sorrow!
Oh, this is a door to beauty closed:
to beg a son to suffer, and for the wind
to offer dahlias of a sleeping moon!
These two teeming springs I have
of warm milk are in the closeness
of my flesh two rhythms of a horse's gallop,
to make vibrate the branch of my anguish.
Oh, breasts, blind beneath my clothes!
Oh, doves with neither eyes nor whiteness!

Oh, what pain of imprisoned blood
is nailing wasps at my brain's base!
But you must come, sweet love, my baby,
because water gives salt, the earth fruit,
and our wombs guard tender infants,
just as a cloud is sweet with rain.

[*She looks toward the door.*]

María! Why do you hurry past my door so?

MARÍA [*she enters with a child in her arms*]: I hurry by whenever I have the child – since you always weep!

YERMA: Yes, you're right.

[*She takes the child and sits down.*]

MARÍA: It makes me sad that you're envious.

YERMA: It's not envy I feel – it's poverty.

MARÍA: Don't you complain.

YERMA: How can I help complaining when I see you and the other women full of flowers from within, and then see myself useless in the midst of so much beauty!

MARÍA: But you have other things. If you'd listen to me you'd be happy.

YERMA: A farm woman who bears no children is useless – like a hand- ful of thorns – and even bad – even though I may be a part of this wasteland abandoned by the hand of God.

[MARÍA *makes a gesture as if to take the child.*]

Take him. He's happier with you. I guess I don't have a mother's hands.

MARÍA: Why do you say that?

YERMA [*she rises*]: Because I'm tired. Because I'm tired of having them, and not being able to use them on something of my own. For I'm hurt, hurt and humiliated beyond endurance, seeing the wheat ripening, the fountains never ceasing to give water, the sheep bearing hundreds of lambs, the she-dogs; until it seems that the whole countryside rises to show me its tender sleeping young, while I feel two hammer-blows here, instead of the mouth of my child.

MARÍA: I don't like you to talk that way.

YERMA: You women who have children can't think about us who don't! You stay always fresh, with no idea of it, just as anyone swimming in fresh water has no idea of thirst.

MARÍA: I don't want to tell you again what I've always said.

YERMA: Each time I have more desire and less hope.

MARÍA: That's very bad.

YERMA: I'll end up believing I'm my own son. Many nights I go down to feed the oxen – which I never did before, because no woman does it – and when I pass through the darkness of the shed my footsteps sound to me like the footsteps of a man.

MARÍA: Each one of us reasons things out for herself.

YERMA: And in spite of all, I go on hoping in myself. You see how I live!

MARÍA: How are your sisters-in-law?

YERMA: Dead may I be, and without a shroud, if ever I speak a word to them.

MARÍA: And your husband?

YERMA: They are three against me.

MARÍA: What do they think about it?

YERMA: The wildest imaginings; like all people who don't have clear consciences. They think I like another man. They don't know that even if I should like another man, to those of my kind, honour comes first. They're stones in my path, but they don't know that I can be, if I want to, an arroyo's rushing water and sweep them away.

[*The* SECOND GIRL *enters and leaves carrying a piece of bread.*]

MARÍA: Even so, I think your husband still loves you.

YERMA: My husband gives me bread and a house.

MARÍA: What troubles you have to go through! What troubles! But remember the wounds of Our Lord.

[*They are at the door.*]

YERMA [*looking at the child*]: He's awake now.

MARÍA: In a little while he'll start to sing.

YERMA: The same eyes as yours. Did you know that? Have you noticed them?

[*Weeping*]

His eyes are the same as yours!

[YERMA *pushes* MARÍA *gently and she leaves silently.* YERMA *walks toward the door through which her husband left.*]

SECOND GIRL: Sst!

YERMA [*turning*]: What?

SECOND GIRL: I waited till she left. My mother's expecting you.

YERMA: Is she alone?

SECOND GIRL: With two neighbours.

YERMA: Tell them to wait a little.

SECOND GIRL: But, are you really going to go? Aren't you afraid?

YERMA: I'm going to go.

SECOND GIRL: That's up to you!

YERMA: Tell them to wait for me even if it's late!

[VICTOR *enters.*]

VICTOR: Is Juan here?

YERMA: Yes.

SECOND GIRL [*acting the accomplice*]: Well then, I'll bring the blouse later.

YERMA: Whenever you like.

[*The* GIRL *leaves.*]

Sit down.

VICTOR: I'm all right like this.

YERMA [*calling*]: Juan!

VICTOR: I've come to say good-bye.

[*He trembles a little, but his composure returns.*]

YERMA: Are you going with your brothers?

VICTOR: That's what my father wants.

YERMA: He must be old now.

VICTOR: Yes. Very old.

[*Pause.*]

YERMA: You're right to change fields.

VICTOR: All fields are alike.

YERMA: No. I'd like to go very far away.

VICTOR. It's all the same. The same sheep have the same wool.

YERMA: For men, yes; but it's a different thing with women. I never heard a man eating say, 'How good these apples are!' You go to what's yours without bothering over trifles. But for myself, I can say I've grown to hate the water from these wells.

VICTOR: That may be.

[*The stage is in a soft shadow.*]

YERMA: Victor.

VICTOR: Yes?

YERMA: Why are you going away? The people here like you.

VICTOR: I've behaved myself.

[*Pause.*]

YERMA: You always behave yourself. When you were a boy, you carried me once in your arms, do you remember that? One never knows what's going to happen.

VICTOR: Everything changes.

YERMA: Some things never change. There are things shut up behind walls that can't change because nobody hears them.

VICTOR: That's how things are.

[*The* SECOND SISTER *appears and goes slowly toward the door, where she remains fixed, illuminated by the last light of evening.*]

YERMA: But if they came out suddenly and shrieked, they'd fill the world.

VICTOR: Nothing would be gained. The ditch in its place, the sheep in fold, the moon in the sky, and the man with his plough.

YERMA: The great pity is we don't profit from the experience of our elders!

[*The long and melancholy sound of the shepherds' conch-shell horns is heard.*]

VICTOR: The flocks.

JUAN [*enters*]: Are you on your way?

VICTOR: Yes. I want to get through the pass before daybreak.

JUAN: Have you any complaints to make against me?

VICTOR: No. You paid me a good price.

JUAN [*to* YERMA]: I bought his sheep.

YERMA: You did?

VICTOR [*to* YERMA]: They're yours.

YERMA: I didn't know that.

JUAN [*satisfied*]: Well, it's so.

VICTOR: Your husband will see his lands overflowing.

YERMA: The harvest comes to the worker who seeks it.

[*The* SISTER *who was at the door leaves and goes into another room.*]

JUAN: Now we haven't any place to put so many sheep.

YERMA [*darkly*]: The earth is large.

[*Pauses.*]

JUAN: We'll go together as far as the arroyo.

VICTOR: I wish this house the greatest possible happiness.

[*He gives* YERMA *his hand.*]

YERMA: May God hear you! Salud!

[VICTOR *is about to leave, but, at an imperceptible movement from* YERMA, *he turns.*]

VICTOR: Did you say something?

YERMA: Salud, I said.

VICTOR: Thank you.

[*They leave.* YERMA *stands, anguished, looking at her hand that she gave to* VICTOR. *She goes quickly to the left and takes up a shawl.*]

SECOND GIRL [*silently, covering her hand*]: Come, let's go.

YERMA: Come.

[*They leave cautiously. The stage is almost in darkness. The* FIRST SISTER *enters with a lamp that must not give the stage any light other than its own. She goes to one side of the stage looking for* YERMA. *The shepherds' conch-shell horns sound.*]

SISTER-IN-LAW [*in a low voice*]: Yerma!

[*The* OTHER SISTER *enters. They look at each other and go toward the door.*]

SECOND SISTER-IN-LAW [*louder*]: Yerma!

FIRST SISTER-IN-LAW [*going to the door, and in an imperious voice*]: Yerma!

[*The bells and horns of the shepherds are heard. The stage is quite dark.*]

CURTAIN

ACT THREE

SCENE I

The house of DOLORES, *the sorceress. Day is breaking.*
    [*Enter* YERMA *with* DOLORES *and* TWO OLD WOMEN.]

DOLORES: You've been brave.

FIRST OLD WOMAN: There's no force in the world like desire.

SECOND OLD WOMAN: But the cemetery was terribly dark.

DOLORES: Many times I've said these prayers in the cemetery with women who wanted to have a child, and they've all been afraid. All except you.

YERMA: I came because I want a child. I don't believe you're a deceitful woman.

DOLORES: I'm not. May my mouth fill with ants, like the mouths of the dead, if ever I've lied. The last time, I said the prayers with a beggar woman who'd been dry longer than you, and her womb sweetened so beautifully that she had two children down there at the river because there wasn't time to get to the village – and she carried them herself in a diaper for me to take care of.

YERMA: And she was able to walk from the river?

DOLORES: She came; her skirts and shoes drenched with blood – but her face shining.

YERMA: And nothing happened to her?

DOLORES: What could happen to her? God is God.

YERMA: Naturally, God is God. Nothing could happen to her. Just pick up her babies and wash them in fresh water. Animals lick them, don't they? I know a son of my own wouldn't make me sick. I have an idea that women who've recently given birth are as though illumined from within and the children sleep hours and hours on them, hearing that stream of warm milk filling the breasts for them to suckle, for them to play in until they don't want any

132

more, until they lift their heads, 'just a little more, child . . .' – and their faces and chests are covered with the white drops.

DOLORES: You'll have a child now. I can assure you, you will.

YERMA: I'll have one because I must. Or I don't understand the world. Sometimes, when I feel certain I'll never, ever . . . a tide of fire sweeps up through me from my feet and everything seems empty; and the men walking in the streets, the cattle, and the stones, all seem to be made of cotton. And I ask myself: 'Why are they put here?'

FIRST OLD WOMAN: It's all right for a married woman to want children, of course, but if she doesn't have them, why this hunger-ing for them? The important thing in life is to let the years carry us along. I'm not criticizing you. You see how I've helped at the prayers. But what land do you expect to give your son, or what happiness, or what silver chair?

YERMA: I'm not thinking about tomorrow; I'm thinking about today. You're old and you see things now like a book already read. I'm thinking how thirsty I am, and how I don't have any freedom. I want to hold my son in my arms so I'll sleep peacefully. Listen closely, and don't be frightened by what I say: even if I knew my son was later going to torture me and hate me and drag me through the streets by the hair, I'd still be happy at his birth, because it's much better to weep for a live man who stabs us than for this ghost sitting year after year upon my heart.

FIRST OLD WOMAN: You're much too young to listen to advice. But while you wait for God's grace, you ought to take refuge in your husband's love.

YERMA: Ah! You've put your finger in the deepest wound in my flesh!

DOLORES: Your husband's a good man.

YERMA [she rises]: He's good! He's good! But what of it? I wish he were bad. But, no. He goes out with his sheep over his trails, and counts his money at night. When he covers me, he's doing his duty, but I feel a waist cold as a corpse's, and I, who've always hated passionate women, would like to be at that instant a moun-tain of fire.

DOLORES: Yerma!

YERMA: I'm not a shameless married woman, but I know that children are born of a man and a woman. Oh, if only I could have them by myself!

DOLORES: Remember, your husband suffers, too.

YERMA: He doesn't suffer. The trouble is, he doesn't want children!

FIRST OLD WOMAN: Don't say that!

YERMA: I can tell that in his glance, and, since he doesn't want them, he doesn't give them to me. I don't love him; I don't love him, and yet he's my only salvation. By honour and by blood. My only salvation.

FIRST OLD WOMAN [*with fear*]: Day will soon be breaking. You ought to go home.

DOLORES: Before you know it, the flocks will be out, and it wouldn't do for you to be seen alone.

YERMA: I needed this relief. How many times do I repeat the prayers?

DOLORES: The laurel prayer, twice; and at noon, St Anne's prayer. When you feel pregnant, bring me the bushel of wheat you promised me.

FIRST OLD WOMAN: It's starting to lighten over the hills already. Go.

DOLORES: They'll soon start opening the big street doors; you'd best go around by the ditch.

YERMA [*discouraged*]: I don't know why I came!

DOLORES: Are you sorry?

YERMA: No!

DOLORES [*disturbed*]: If you're afraid, I'll go with you to the corner.

FIRST OLD WOMAN [*uneasily*]: It'll just be daylight when you reach home.

[*Voices are heard.*]

DOLORES: Quiet.

[*They listen.*]

FIRST OLD WOMAN: It's nobody. God go with you.

[YERMA *starts toward the door, but at this moment a knock is heard. The* THREE WOMEN *are standing.*]

DOLORES: Who is it?

VOICE: It's me.

YERMA: Open the door.

   [DOLORES *is reluctant.*]

   Will you open or not?

   [*Whispering is heard.* JUAN *enters with the* TWO SISTERS.]

SECOND SISTER-IN-LAW: Here she is.

YERMA: Here I am.

JUAN: What are you doing in this place? If I could shout I'd wake up the whole village so they'd see where the good name of my house has gone to; but I have to swallow everything and keep quiet – because you're my wife.

YERMA: I too would shout, if I could, so that even the dead would rise and see the innocence that covers me.

JUAN: No, don't tell me that! I can stand everything but that. You deceive me; you trick me, and since I'm a man who works in the fields, I'm no match for your cleverness.

DOLORES: Juan!

JUAN: You, not a word out of you!

DOLORES [*strongly*]: Your wife has done nothing wrong.

JUAN: She's been doing it from the very day of the wedding. Looking at me with two needles, passing wakeful nights with her eyes open at my side, and filling my pillows with evil sighs.

YERMA: Be quiet!

JUAN: And I can't stand any more. Because one would have to be made of iron to put up with a woman who wants to stick her fingers into your heart and who goes out of her house at night. In search of what? Tell me! There aren't any flowers to pick in the streets.

YERMA: I won't let you say another word. Not one word more. You and your people imagine you're the only ones who look out for honour, and you don't realize my people have never had anything to conceal. Come on now. Come near and smell my clothes. Come close! See if you can find an odour that's not yours, that's not from your body. Stand me naked in the middle of the square and spit on me. Do what you want with me, since I'm your wife, but take care not to set a man's name in my breast.

JUAN: I'm not the one who sets it there. You do it by your conduct, and the town's beginning to say so. It's beginning to say it openly. When I come on a group, they all fall silent; when I go to weigh the flour, they all fall silent, and even at night, in the fields, when I awaken, it seems to me that the branches of the trees become silent too.

YERMA: I don't know why the evil winds that soil the wheat begin – but look you and see if the wheat is good!

JUAN: Nor do I know what a woman is looking for outside her house at all hours.

YERMA [bursting out, embracing her husband]: I'm looking for you. I'm looking for you. It's you I look for day and night without finding a shade where to draw breath. It's your blood and help I want.

JUAN: Stay away from me.

YERMA: Don't put me away – love me!

JUAN: Get away!

YERMA: Look how I'm left alone! As if the moon searched for herself in the sky. Look at me!

[She looks at him.]

JUAN [he looks at her and draws away roughly]: Let me be – once and for all!

DOLORES: Juan!

[YERMA falls to the floor.]

YERMA [loudly]: When I went out looking for my flowers, I ran into a wall. Ay-y-y! Ay-y-y! It's against that wall I'll break my head.

JUAN: Be quiet. Let's go.

DOLORES: Good God!

YERMA [shouting]: Cursed be my father who left me his blood of a father of a hundred sons. Cursed be my blood that searches for them, knocking against walls.

JUAN: I told you to be quiet!

DOLORES: People are coming! Speak lower.

YERMA: I don't care. At least let my voice go free, now that I'm entering the darkest part of the pit.

[*She rises.*]

At least let this beautiful thing come out of my body and fill the air.

[*Voices are heard.*]

DOLORES: They're going to pass by here.

JUAN: Silence.

YERMA: That's it! That's it! Silence. Never fear.

JUAN: Let's go. Quick!

YERMA: That's it! That's it! And it's no use for me to wring my hands! It's one thing to wish with one's head . . .

JUAN: Be still!

YERMA [*low*]: It's one thing to wish with one's head and another for the body – cursed be the body! – not to respond. It's written, and I'm not going to raise my arms against the sea. That's it! Let my mouth be struck dumb!

[*She leaves.*]

QUICK CURTAIN

ACT THREE

SCENE 2

Environs of a hermitage high in the mountains. Downstage are the wheels of a cart and some canvas forming the rustic tent where YERMA *is.*

[*Some women enter carrying offerings for the shrine. They are barefoot. The happy* OLD WOMAN *of the first act is on the stage.*]

[*Heard while the curtain is still closed*]
> You I never could see
> when you were fancy free,
> but now that you're a wife
> I'll find you, yes,
> and take off your dress,
> you, pilgrim and a wife
> when night is dark all round,
> when midnight starts to sound.

OLD WOMAN [*lazily*]: Have you already drunk the holy water?

FIRST WOMAN: Yes.

OLD WOMAN: Now let's see this saint work.

FIRST WOMAN: We believe in him.

OLD WOMAN: You come to ask the saint for children, and it just happens that every year more single men come on this pilgrimage too; what's going on here?

[*She laughs.*]

FIRST WOMAN: Why do you come here if you don't believe in him?

OLD WOMAN: To see what goes on. I'm just crazy to see what goes on. And to watch out for my son. Last year two men killed themselves over a barren wife, and I want to be on guard. And lastly, I come because I feel like it.

FIRST WOMAN: May God forgive you!

[*She leaves.*]

OLD WOMAN [*sarcastically*]: May He forgive you!

[*She leaves.* MARÍA *enters with the* FIRST GIRL.]

FIRST GIRL: Did she come?

MARÍA: There's her cart. It was hard work to make them come. She's been a month without getting up from her chair. I'm afraid of her. She has some idea I don't understand, but it's a bad idea.

FIRST GIRL: I came with my sister. She's been coming here eight years in vain.

MARÍA: The one who's meant to have children, has them.

FIRST GIRL: That's what I say.

[*Voices are heard.*]

MARÍA: I've never liked these pilgrimages. Let's get down to the farms where there are some people around.

FIRST GIRL: Last year, when it got dark, some young men pinched my sister's breasts.

MARÍA: For four leagues round nothing is heard but these terrible stories.

FIRST GIRL: I saw more than forty barrels of wine back of the hermitage.

MARÍA: A river of single men comes down these mountains.

[*They leave. Voices are heard.* YERMA *enters with* SIX WOMEN *who are going to the chapel. They are barefooted and carry decorated candles. Night begins to fall.*]

MARÍA:

> Lord, make blossom the rose,
> leave not my rose in shadow.

SECOND WOMAN:

> Upon her barren flesh
> make blossom the yellow rose.

MARÍA:

> And in your servants' wombs
> the dark flame of the earth.

CHORUS OF WOMEN:

> Lord, make blossom the rose,
> leave not my rose in shadow.

[*They kneel.*]

YERMA:

> The sky must have such gardens
> with rose trees of its joy,
> between the rose and the rose,
> one rose of all the wonder.
> Bright flash of dawn appears,
> and an archangel guards,
> his wings like storms outspread,
> his eyes like agonies.
> While sweet about its leaves
> the streams of warm milk play,
> play and wet the faces
> of the tranquil stars.
> Lord, make your rose tree bloom
> upon my barren flesh.

[*They rise.*]

SECOND WOMAN:

> Lord, with your own hand soothe
> the thorns upon her cheek.

YERMA:

> Hark to me, penitent
> in holy pilgrimage.
> Open your rose in my flesh
> though thousand thorns it have.

CHORUS OF WOMEN:

> Lord, make blossom the rose,
> leave not my rose in shadow.

YERMA:

> Upon my barren flesh
> one rose of all the wonder.

[*They leave.*]

[GIRLS *running with long garlands in their hands appear from the left. On the right, three others, looking backward. On the stage there is something like a crescendo of voices and harness bells, and bellringers'*

collars. Higher up appear the SEVEN GIRLS *who wave the garlands to-*
ward the left. The noise increases and the two traditional MASKS
appear. One is Male and the other Female. They carry large masks.
They are not in any fashion grotesque, but of great beauty and with a
feeling of pure earth. The Female shakes a collar of large bells. The
back of the stage fills with people who shout and comment on the
dance. It has grown quite dark.]

CHILDREN: The devil and his wife! The devil and his wife!

FEMALE:

> In the wilderness stream
> the sad wife was bathing.
> About her body crept
> the little water snails.
> The sand upon the banks,
> and the little morning breeze
> made her laughter sparkle
> and her shoulders shiver.
> Ah, how naked stood
> the maiden in the stream!

BOY:

> Ah, how the maiden wept!

FIRST MAN:

> Oh, wife bereft of love
> in the wind and water!

SECOND MAN:

> Let her say for whom she longs!

FIRST MAN:

> Let her say for whom she waits!

SECOND MAN:

> Ah, with her withered womb
> and her colour shattered!

FEMALE:

> When night-tide falls I'll tell,
> when night-tide glowing falls.

In the night-tide of the pilgrimage
I'll tear my ruffled skirt.

BOY:

Then quickly night-tide fell.
Oh, how the night was falling!
See how dark becomes
the mountain waterfall.

[*Guitars begin to sound.*]

MALE [*he rises and shakes the horn*]:

Ah, how white
the sorrowing wife!
Ah, how she sighs beneath the branches!
Poppy and carnation you'll later be
when the male spreads out his cape.

[*He approaches.*]

If you come to the pilgrimage
to pray your womb may flower
don't wear a mourning veil
but a gown of fine Dutch linen.
Walk alone along the walls
where fig trees thickest grow
and bear my earthly body
until the white dawn wails.
Ah, how she shines!
How she was shining,
ah, how the sad wife sways!

FEMALE:

Ah, let love place on her
wreaths and coronets,
let darts of brightest gold
be fastened in her breast.

MALE:

Seven times she wept
and nine she rose,

fifteen times they joined
jasmines with oranges.

THIRD MAN:

Strike her now with the horn!

SECOND MAN:

With both the rose and the dance!

FIRST MAN:

Ah, how the wife is swaying!

MALE:

In this pilgrimage
the man commands always.
Husbands are bulls.
The man commands always
and women are flowers,
for him who wins them.

BOY:

Strike her now with the wind!

SECOND MAN:

Strike her now with the branch!

MALE:

Come and see the splendour
of the wife washed clean!

FIRST MAN:

Like a reed she curves.

MEN:

Let young girls draw away!

MALE:

Let the dance burn.
And the shining body
of the immaculate wife.

[*They disappear dancing amidst smiles and the sound of beating palms.
They sing.*]

The sky must have such gardens
with rose trees of its joy,

between the rose and the rose
one rose of all the wonder.

[TWO GIRLS *pass again, shouting. The happy* OLD WOMAN *enters.*]

OLD WOMAN: Let's see if you'll let us sleep now. But pretty soon it'll be something else.

[YERMA *enters.*]

You.

[YERMA *is downcast and does not speak.*]

Tell me, what did you come here for?

YERMA: I don't know.

OLD WOMAN: Aren't you sure yet? Where's your husband?

[YERMA *gives signs of fatigue and acts like a person whose head is bursting with a fixed idea.*]

YERMA: He's there.

OLD WOMAN: What's he doing?

YERMA: Drinking.

[*Pause. Putting her hands to her forehead.*]

Ay-y-y!

OLD WOMAN: Ay-y, ay-y! Less 'ay!' and more spirit. I couldn't tell you anything before, but now I can.

YERMA: What can you tell me that I don't know already?

OLD WOMAN: What can no longer be hushed up. What shouts from all the rooftops. The fault is your husband's. Do you hear? He can cut off my hands if it isn't. Neither his father, nor his grandfather, nor his great-grandfather behaved like men of good blood. For them to have a son heaven and earth had to meet – because they're nothing but spit. But not your people. You have brothers and cousins for a hundred miles around. Just see what a curse has fallen on your loveliness.

YERMA: A curse. A puddle of poison on the wheat heads.

OLD WOMAN: But you have feet to leave your house.

YERMA: To leave?

OLD WOMAN: When I saw you in the pilgrimage, my heart gave a start. Women come here to know new men. And the saint performs the miracle. My son's there behind the chapel waiting for me. My house needs a woman. Go with him and the three of us will live together. My son's made of blood. Like me. If you come to my house, there'll still be the odour of cradles. The ashes from your bedcovers will be bread and salt for your children. Come, don't you worry about what people will say. And as for your husband, in my house there are stout hearts and strong weapons to keep him from even crossing the street.

YERMA: Hush, hush! It's not that. I'd never do it. I can't just go out looking for someone. Do you imagine I could know another man? Where would that leave my honour? Water can't run up-hill, nor does the full moon rise at noonday. On the road I've started, I'll stay. Did you really think I could submit to another man? That I could go asking for what's mine, like a slave? Look at me, so you'll know me and never speak to me again. I'm not looking for anyone.

OLD WOMAN: When one's thirsty, one's grateful for water.

YERMA: I'm like a dry field where a thousand pairs of oxen plough, and you offer me a little glass of well water. Mine is a sorrow already beyond the flesh.

OLD WOMAN [strongly]: Then stay that way – if you want to! Like the thistles in a dry field, pinched, barren!

YERMA [strongly]: Barren, yes, I know it! Barren! You don't have to throw it in my face. Nor come to amuse yourself, as youngsters do, in the suffering of a tiny animal. Ever since I married, I've been avoiding that word, and this is the first time I've heard it, the first time it's been said to my face. The first time I see it's the truth.

OLD WOMAN: You make me feel no pity. None. I'll find another woman for my boy.

[She leaves. A great chorus is heard distantly, sung by the pilgrims. YERMA goes toward the cart, and from behind it JUAN appears.]

YERMA: Were you there all the time?

JUAN: I was.

YERMA: Spying?

JUAN: Spying.

YERMA: And you heard?

JUAN: Yes.

YERMA: And so? Leave me and go to the singing.

[*She sits on the canvases.*]

JUAN: It's time I spoke, too.

YERMA: Speak!

JUAN: And complained.

YERMA: About what?

JUAN: I have a bitterness in my throat.

YERMA: And I in my bones.

JUAN: This is the last time I'll put up with your continual lament for dark things, outside of life – for things in the air.

YERMA [*with dramatic surprise*]: Outside of life, you say? In the air, you say?

JUAN: For things that haven't happened and that neither you nor I can control.

YERMA [*violently*]: Go on! Go on!

JUAN: For things that don't matter to me. You hear that? That don't matter to me. Now I'm forced to tell you. What matters to me is what I can hold in my hands. What my eyes can see.

YERMA [*rising to her knees, desperately*]: Yes, yes. That's what I wanted to hear from your lips . . . the truth isn't felt when it's inside us, but how great it is, how it shouts when it comes out and raises its arms! It doesn't matter to him! Now I've heard it!

JUAN [*coming near her*]: Tell yourself it had to happen like this. Listen to me.

[*He embraces her to help her rise.*]

Many women would be glad to have your life. Without children life is sweeter. I am happy not having them. It's not your fault.

YERMA: Then what did you want with me?

JUAN: Yourself!

YERMA [*excitedly*]: True! You wanted a home, ease, and a woman. But nothing more. Is what I say true?

JUAN: It's true. Like everyone.

YERMA: And what about the rest? What about your son?

JUAN [*strongly*]: Didn't you hear me say I don't care? Don't ask me any more about it! Do I have to shout in your ear so you'll understand and perhaps live in peace now!

YERMA: And you never thought about it, even when you saw I wanted one?

JUAN: Never.

[*Both are on the ground.*]

YERMA: And I'm not to hope for one?

JUAN: No.

YERMA: Nor you?

JUAN: Nor I. Resign yourself!

YERMA: Barren!

JUAN: And lie in peace. You and I – happily, peacefully. Embrace me!

[*He embraces her.*]

YERMA: What are you looking for?

JUAN: You. In the moonlight you're beautiful.

YERMA: You want me as you sometimes want a pigeon to eat.

JUAN: Kiss me . . . like this.

YERMA: That I'll never do. Never.

[*YERMA gives a shriek and seizes her husband by the throat. He falls backward. She chokes him until he dies. The chorus of the pilgrimage begins.*]

YERMA: Barren, barren, but sure. Now I really know it for sure. And alone.

[*She rises. People begin to gather.*]

Now I'll sleep without startling myself awake, anxious to see if I feel in my blood another new blood. My body dry for ever! What do you want? Don't come near me, because I've killed my son. I myself have killed my son!

[*A group that remains in the background, gathers. The chorus of the pilgrimage is heard.*]

CURTAIN

THE HOUSE OF
BERNARDA ALBA

*A Drama about Women in
the Villages of Spain*

Characters

—

BERNARDA (*age: 60*)
MARÍA JOSEFA, *Bernarda's Mother* (*age: 80*)
ANGUSTIAS, *Bernarda's Daughter* (*age: 39*)
MAGDALENA, *Bernarda's Daughter* (*age: 30*)
AMELIA, *Bernarda's Daughter* (*age: 27*)
MARTIRIO, *Bernarda's Daughter* (*age: 24*)
ADELA, *Bernarda's Daughter* (*age: 20*)
A MAID (*age: 50*)
LA PONCIA, *A Maid* (*age: 60*)
PRUDENCIA (*age: 50*)
WOMEN IN MOURNING

*The writer states that these Three Acts are intended
as a photographic document.*

ACT ONE

A very white room in BERNARDA ALBA'S *house. The walls are white. There are arched doorways with jute curtains tied back with tassels and ruffles. Wicker chairs. On the walls, pictures of unlikely landscapes full of nymphs or legendary kings.*

> [*It is summer. A great brooding silence fills the stage. It is empty when the curtain rises. Bells can be heard tolling outside.*]

FIRST SERVANT [*entering*]: The tolling of those bells hits me right between the eyes.

PONCIA [*she enters, eating bread and sausage*]: More than two hours of mumbo-jumbo. Priests are here from all the towns. The church looks beautiful. At the first responsory for the dead, Magdalena fainted.

FIRST SERVANT: She's the one who's left most alone.

PONCIA: She's the only one who loved her father. Ay! Thank God we're alone for a little. I came over to eat.

FIRST SERVANT: If Bernarda sees you . . . !

PONCIA: She's not eating today so she'd just as soon we'd all die of hunger! Domineering old tyrant! But she'll be fooled! I opened the sausage crock.

FIRST SERVANT [*with an anxious sadness*]: Couldn't you give me some for my little girl, Poncia?

PONCIA: Go ahead! And take a fistful of peas too. She won't know the difference today.

VOICE [*within*]: Bernarda!

PONCIA: There's the grandmother! Isn't she locked up tight?

FIRST SERVANT: Two turns of the key.

PONCIA: You'd better put the cross-bar up too. She's got the fingers of a lock-picker!

VOICE [*within*]: Bernarda!

PONCIA [*shouting*]: She's coming!

> [*To the* SERVANT]

Clean everything up good. If Bernarda doesn't find things shining, she'll pull out the few hairs I have left.

SERVANT: What a woman!

PONCIA: Tyrant over everyone around her. She's perfectly capable of sitting on your heart and watching you die for a whole year without turning off that cold little smile she wears on her wicked face. Scrub, scrub those dishes!

SERVANT: I've got blood on my hands from so much polishing of everything.

PONCIA: She's the cleanest, she's the decentest, she's the highest everything! A good rest her poor husband's earned!

[*The bells stop.*]

SERVANT: Did all the relatives come?

PONCIA: Just hers. His people hate her. They came to see him dead and make the sign of the cross over him; that's all.

SERVANT: Are there enough chairs?

PONCIA: More than enough. Let them sit on the floor. When Bernarda's father died people stopped coming under this roof. She doesn't want them to see her in her 'domain'. Curse her!

SERVANT: She's been good to you.

PONCIA: Thirty years washing her sheets. Thirty years eating her leftovers. Nights of watching when she had a cough. Whole days peeking through a crack in the shutters to spy on the neighbours and carry her the tale. Life without secrets one from the other. But in spite of that – curse her! May the 'pain of the piercing nail' strike her in the eyes.

SERVANT: Poncia!

PONCIA: But I'm a good watchdog! I bark when I'm told and bite beggars' heels when she sics me on 'em. My sons work in her fields – both of them already married, but one of these days I'll have enough.

SERVANT: And then ... ?

PONCIA: Then I'll lock myself up in a room with her and spit in her face – a whole year. 'Bernarda, here's for this, that and the other!' Till I leave her – just like a lizard the boys have squashed.

For that's what she is – she and her whole family! Not that I envy her her life. Five girls are left her, five ugly daughters – not counting Angustias, the eldest, by her first husband, who has money – the rest of them, plenty of eyelets to embroider, plenty of linen petticoats, but bread and grapes when it comes to inheritance.

SERVANT: Well, *I'd* like to have what they've got!

PONCIA: All we have is our hands and a hole in God's earth.

SERVANT: And that's the only earth they'll ever leave to us – to us who have nothing!

PONCIA [*at the cupboard*]: The glass has some specks.

SERVANT: Neither soap nor rag will take them off.

[*The bells toll.*]

PONCIA: The last prayer! I'm going over and listen. I certainly like the way our priest sings. In the Pater Noster his voice went up, and up – like a pitcher filling with water little by little. Of course, at the end his voice cracked, but it's glorious to hear it. No, there never was anybody like the old Sacristan – Tronchapinos. At my mother's Mass, may she rest in peace, he sang. The walls shook – and when he said 'Amen', it was as if a wolf had come into the church.

[*Imitating him*]

A-a-a-a-men!

[*She starts coughing.*]

SERVANT: Watch out – you'll strain your windpipe!

PONCIA: I'd rather strain something else!

[*Goes out laughing.*]

[*The* SERVANT *scrubs. The bells toll.*]

SERVANT [*imitating the bells*]: Dong, dong, dong. Dong, dong, dong. May God forgive him!

BEGGAR WOMAN [*at the door, with a little girl*]: Blesséd be God!

SERVANT: Dong, dong, dong. I hope he waits many years for us! Dong, dong, dong.

BEGGAR [*loudly, a little annoyed*]: Blesséd be God!

SERVANT [*annoyed*]: For ever and ever!

BEGGAR: I came for the scraps.

153

[*The bells stop tolling.*]

SERVANT: You can go right out the way you came in. Today's scraps are for me.

BEGGAR: But you have somebody to take care of you – and my little girl and I are all alone!

SERVANT: Dogs are alone too, and they live.

BEGGAR: They always give them to me.

SERVANT: Get out of here! Who let you in anyway? You've already tracked up the place.

[*The* BEGGAR WOMAN *and* LITTLE GIRL *leave. The* SERVANT *goes on scrubbing.*]

Floors finished with oil, cupboards, pedestals, iron beds – but us servants, we can suffer in silence – and live in mud huts with a plate and a spoon. I hope some day not a one will be left to tell it.

[*The bells sound again.*]

Yes, yes – ring away. Let them put you in a coffin with gold inlay and brocade to carry it on – you're no less dead than I'll be, so take what's coming to you, Antonio María Benavides – stiff in your broadcloth suit and your high boots – take what's coming to you! You'll never again lift my skirts behind the corral door!

[*From the rear door, two by two,* WOMEN IN MOURNING *with large shawls and black skirts and fans, begin to enter. They come in slowly until the stage is full.*]

SERVANT [*breaking into a wail*]: Oh, Antonio María Benavides, now you'll never see these walls, nor break bread in this house again! I'm the one who loved you most of all your servants.

[*Pulling her hair*]

Must I live on after you've gone? Must I go on living?

[*The two hundred women finish coming in, and* BERNARDA *and her five* DAUGHTERS *enter.* BERNARDA *leans on a cane.*]

BERNARDA [*to the* SERVANT]: Silence!

SERVANT [*weeping*]: Bernarda!

BERNARDA: Less shrieking and more work. You should have had all this cleaner for the wake. Get out. This isn't your place.

[*The* SERVANT *goes off crying.*]

The poor are like animals – they seem to be made of different stuff.

FIRST WOMAN: The poor feel their sorrows too.

BERNARDA: But they forget them in front of a plateful of peas.

FIRST GIRL [*timidly*]: Eating is necessary for living.

BERNARDA: At your age one doesn't talk in front of older people.

WOMAN: Be quiet, child.

BERNARDA: I've never taken lessons from anyone. Sit down.

 [*They sit down. Pause. Loudly*]

Magdalena, don't cry. If you want to cry, get under your bed. Do you hear me?

SECOND WOMAN [*to* BERNARDA]: Have you started to work the fields?

BERNARDA: Yesterday.

THIRD WOMAN: The sun comes down like lead.

FIRST WOMAN: I haven't known heat like this for years.

 [*Pause. They all fan themselves.*]

BERNARDA: Is the lemonade ready?

PONCIA: Yes, Bernarda.

 [*She brings in a large tray full of little white jars which she distributes.*]

BERNARDA: Give the men some.

PONCIA: They're already drinking in the patio.

BERNARDA: Let them get out the way they came in. I don't want them walking through here.

A GIRL [*to* ANGUSTIAS]: Pepe el Romano was with the men during the service.

ANGUSTIAS: There he was.

BERNARDA: His mother was there. She saw his mother. Neither she nor I saw Pepe . . .

GIRL: I thought . . .

BERNARDA: The one who *was* there was Darajalí, the widower. Very close to your Aunt. We all of us saw him.

SECOND WOMAN [*aside, in a low voice*]: Wicked, worse than wicked woman!

THIRD WOMAN: A tongue like a knife!

BERNARDA: Women in church shouldn't look at any man but the priest – and him only because he wears skirts. To turn your head is to be looking for the warmth of corduroy.

FIRST WOMAN: Sanctimonious old snake!

PONCIA [*between her teeth*]: Itching for a man's warmth.

BERNARDA [*beating with her cane on the floor*]: Blesséd be God!

ALL [*crossing themselves*]: For ever blesséd and praised.

BERNARDA: Rest in peace with holy company at your head.

ALL: Rest in peace!

BERNARDA: With the Angel Saint Michael, and his sword of justice.

ALL: Rest in peace.

BERNARDA: With the key that opens, and the hand that locks.

ALL: Rest in peace.

BERNARDA: With the most blesséd, and the little lights of the field.

ALL: Rest in peace!

BERNARDA: With our holy charity, and all souls on land and sea.

ALL: Rest in peace!

BERNARDA: Grant rest to your servant, Antonio María Benavides, and give him the crown of your blesséd glory.

ALL: Amen.

BERNARDA [*she rises and chants*]: Requiem aeternam dona eis domine.

ALL [*standing and chanting in the Gregorian fashion*]: Et lux perpetua luceat eis.

　　[*They cross themselves.*]

FIRST WOMAN: May you have health to pray for his soul.

　　[*They start filing out.*]

THIRD WOMAN: You won't lack loaves of hot bread.

SECOND WOMAN: Nor a roof for your daughters.

　　[*They are all filing in front of* BERNARDA *and going out.*]

　　[ANGUSTIAS *leaves by the door to the patio.*]

FOURTH WOMAN: May you go on enjoying your wedding wheat.

PONCIA [*she enters, carrying a money-bag*]: From the men – this bag of money for Masses.

BERNARDA: Thank them – and let them have a glass of brandy.

GIRL [*to* MAGDALENA]: Magdalena . . .

BERNARDA [*to* MAGDALENA, *who is starting to cry*]: Sh-h-h-h!
[*She beats with her cane on the floor.*
All the women have gone out.]

BERNARDA [*to the women who have just left*]: Go back to your houses and criticize everything you've seen! I hope it'll be many years before you pass under the archway of my door again.

PONCIA: You've nothing to complain about. The whole town came.

BERNARDA: Yes, to fill my house with the sweat from their wraps and the poison of their tongues.

AMELIA: Mother, don't talk like that.

BERNARDA: What other way is there to talk about this curséd village with no river – this village full of wells where you drink water always fearful it's been poisoned?

PONCIA: Look what they've done to the floor!

BERNARDA: As though a herd of goats had passed through.
[PONCIA *cleans the floor.*]
Adela, give me a fan.

ADELA: Take this one.
[*She gives her a round fan with green and red flowers.*]

BERNARDA [*throwing the fan on the floor*]: Is that the fan to give to a widow? Give me a black one and learn to respect your father's memory.

MARTIRIO: Take mine.

BERNARDA: And you?

MARTIRIO: I'm not hot.

BERNARDA: Well, look for another, because you'll need it. For the eight years of mourning, not a breath of air will get in this house from the street. We'll act as if we'd sealed up doors and windows with bricks. That's what happened in my father's house – and in my grandfather's house. Meantime, you can all start embroidering your hope-chest linens. I have twenty bolts of linen in the chest from which to cut sheets and coverlets. Magdalena can embroider them.

MAGDALENA: It's all the same to me.

ADELA [*sourly*]: If you don't want to embroider them – they can go
without. That way yours will look better.

MAGDALENA: Neither mine nor yours. I know I'm not going to
marry. I'd rather carry sacks to the mill. Anything except sit here
day after day in this dark room.

BERNARDA: That's what a woman is for.

MAGDALENA: Cursed be all women.

BERNARDA: In this house you'll do what I order. You can't run with
the story to your father any more. Needle and thread for women.
Whiplash and mules for men. That's the way it has to be for people
who have certain obligations.

[ADELA *goes out.*]

VOICE: Bernarda! Let me out!

BERNARDA [*calling*]: Let her out now!

[*The* FIRST SERVANT *enters.*]

FIRST SERVANT: I had a hard time holding her. In spite of her eighty
years, your mother's strong as an oak.

BERNARDA: It runs in the family. My grandfather was the same way.

SERVANT: Several times during the wake I had to cover her mouth
with an empty sack because she wanted to shout out to you to
give her dishwater to drink at least, and some dogmeat, which is
what she says you feed her.

MARTIRIO: She's mean!

BERNARDA [*to* SERVANT]: Let her get some fresh air in the patio.

SERVANT: She took her rings and the amethyst earrings out of the
box, put them on, and told me she wants to get married.

[*The* DAUGHTERS *laugh.*]

BERNARDA: Go with her and be careful she doesn't get near the well.

SERVANT: You don't need to be afraid she'll jump in.

BERNARDA: It's not that – but the neighbours can see her there from
their windows.

[*The* SERVANT *leaves.*]

MARTIRIO: We'll go change our clothes.

BERNARDA: Yes, but don't take the kerchiefs from your heads.

[ADELA *enters.*]

And Angustias?

ADELA [*meaningfully*]: I saw her looking out through the cracks of the back door. The men had just gone.

BERNARDA: And you, what were *you* doing at the door?

ADELA: I went there to see if the hens had laid.

BERNARDA: But the men had already gone!

ADELA [*meaningfully*]: A group of them were still standing outside.

BERNARDA [*furiously*]: Angustias! Angustias!

ANGUSTIAS [*entering*]: Did you want something?

BERNARDA: For what – and at whom – were you looking?

ANGUSTIAS: Nobody.

BERNARDA: Is it decent for a woman of your class to be running after a man the day of her father's funeral? Answer me! Whom were you looking at?

[*Pause.*]

ANGUSTIAS: I . . .

BERNARDA: Yes, you!

ANGUSTIAS: Nobody.

BERNARDA: Soft! Honeytongue!

[*She strikes her.*]

PONCIA [*running to her*]: Bernarda, calm down!

[*She holds her.* ANGUSTIAS *weeps.*]

BERNARDA: Get out of here, all of you!

[*They all go out.*]

PONCIA: She did it not realizing what she was doing – although it's bad, of course. It really disgusted me to see her sneak along to the patio. Then she stood at the window listening to the men's talk which, as usual, was not the sort one should listen to.

BERNARDA: That's what they come to funerals for.

[*With curiosity*]

What were they talking about?

PONCIA: They were talking about Paca la Roseta. Last night they tied her husband up in a stall, stuck her on a horse behind the saddle, and carried her away to the depths of the olive grove.

BERNARDA: And what did she do?

PONCIA: She? She was just as happy – they say her breasts were exposed and Maximiliano held on to her as if he were playing a guitar. Terrible!

BERNARDA: And what happened?

PONCIA: What had to happen. They came back almost at daybreak. Paca la Roseta with her hair loose and a wreath of flowers on her head.

BERNARDA: She's the only bad woman we have in the village.

PONCIA: Because she's not from here. She's from far away. And those who went with her are the sons of outsiders too. The men from here aren't up to a thing like that.

BERNARDA: No, but they like to see it, and talk about it, and suck their fingers over it.

PONCIA: They were saying a lot more things.

BERNARDA [looking from side to side with a certain fear]: What things?

PONCIA: I'm ashamed to talk about them.

BERNARDA: And my daughter heard them?

PONCIA: Of course!

BERNARDA: That one takes after her aunts: white and mealy-mouthed and casting sheep's eyes at any little barber's compliment. Oh, what one has to go through and put up with so people will be decent and not too wild!

PONCIA: It's just that your daughters are of an age when they ought to have husbands. Mighty little trouble they give you. Angustias must be much more than thirty now.

BERNARDA: Exactly thirty-nine.

PONCIA: Imagine. And she's never had a beau . . .

BERNARDA [furiously]: None of them has ever had a beau and they've never needed one! They get along very well.

PONCIA: I didn't mean to offend you.

BERNARDA: For a hundred miles around there's no one good enough to come near them. The men in this town are not of their class. Do you want me to turn them over to the first shepherd?

PONCIA: You should have moved to another town.

BERNARDA: That's it. To sell them!

PONCIA: No, Bernarda, to change. . . . Of course, any place else, they'd be the poor ones.

BERNARDA: Hold your tormenting tongue!

PONCIA: One can't even talk to you. Do we, or do we not share secrets?

BERNARDA: We do not. You're a servant and I pay you. Nothing more.

PONCIA: But . . .

FIRST SERVANT [*entering*]: Don Arturo's here. He's come to see about dividing the inheritance.

BERNARDA: Let's go.

    [*To the* SERVANT]

You start whitewashing the patio.

    [*To* PONCIA]

And you start putting all the dead man's clothes away in the chest.

PONCIA: We could give away some of the things.

BERNARDA: Nothing – not a button even! Not even the cloth we covered his face with.

    [*She goes out slowly, leaning on her cane. At the door she turns to look at the* TWO SERVANTS. *They go out. She leaves.*]

    [AMELIA *and* MARTIRIO *enter.*]

AMELIA: Did you take the medicine?

MARTIRIO: For all the good it'll do me.

AMELIA: But you took it?

MARTIRIO: I do things without any faith, but like clockwork.

AMELIA: Since the new doctor came you look livelier.

MARTIRIO: I feel the same.

AMELIA: Did you notice? Adelaida wasn't at the funeral.

MARTIRIO: I know. Her sweetheart doesn't let her go out even to the front doorstep. Before, she was gay. Now, not even powder on her face.

AMELIA: These days a girl doesn't know whether to have a beau or not.

MARTIRIO: It's all the same.

AMELIA: The whole trouble is all these wagging tongues that won't let us live. Adelaida has probably had a bad time.

MARTIRIO: She's afraid of our mother. Mother is the only one who knows the story of Adelaida's father and where he got his lands. Every time she comes here, Mother twists the knife in the wound. Her father killed his first wife's husband in Cuba so he could marry her himself. Then he left her there and went off with another woman who already had one daughter, and then he took up with this other girl, Adelaida's mother, and married her after his second wife died insane.

AMELIA: But why isn't a man like that put in jail?

MARTIRIO: Because men help each other cover up things like that and no one's able to tell on them.

AMELIA: But Adelaida's not to blame for any of that.

MARTIRIO: No. But history repeats itself. I can see that everything is a terrible repetition. And she'll have the same fate as her mother and grandmother – both of them wife to the man who fathered her.

AMELIA: What an awful thing!

MARTIRIO: It's better never to look at a man. I've been afraid of them since I was a little girl. I'd see them in the yard, yoking the oxen and lifting grain sacks, shouting and stamping, and I was always afraid to grow up for fear one of them would suddenly take me in his arms. God has made me weak and ugly and has definitely put such things away from me.

AMELIA: Don't say that! Enrique Humanas was after you and he liked you.

MARTIRIO: That was just people's ideas! One time I stood in my nightgown at the window until daybreak because he let me know through his shepherd's little girl that he was going to come, and he didn't. It was all just talk. Then he married someone else who had more money than I.

AMELIA: And ugly as the devil.

MARTIRIO: What do men care about ugliness? All they care about is lands, yokes of oxen, and a submissive bitch who'll feed them.

AMELIA: Ay!

[MAGDALENA *enters.*]

MAGDALENA: What are you doing?

MARTIRIO: Just here.

AMELIA: And you?

MAGDALENA: I've been going through all the rooms. Just to walk a little, and look at Grandmother's needlepoint pictures – the little woollen dog, and the black man wrestling with the lion – which we liked so much when we were children. Those were happier times. A wedding lasted ten days and evil tongues weren't in style. Today people are more refined. Brides wear white veils, just as in the cities, and we drink bottled wine, but we rot inside because of what people might say.

MARTIRIO: Lord knows what went on then!

AMELIA [*to* MAGDALENA]: One of your shoelaces has come untied.

MAGDALENA: What of it?

AMELIA: You'll step on it and fall.

MAGDALENA: One less!

MARTIRIO: And Adela?

MAGDALENA: Ah! She put on the green dress she made to wear for her birthday, went out to the yard, and began shouting: 'Chickens! Chickens, look at me!' I had to laugh.

AMELIA: If Mother had only seen her!

MAGDALENA: Poor little thing! She's the youngest one of us and still has her illusions. I'd give something to see her happy.

[*Pause.* ANGUSTIAS *crosses the stage, carrying some towels.*]

ANGUSTIAS: What time is it?

MAGDALENA: It must be twelve.

ANGUSTIAS: So late?

AMELIA: It's about to strike.

[ANGUSTIAS *goes out.*]

MAGDALENA [*meaningfully*]: Do you know what?

[*Pointing after* ANGUSTIAS]

AMELIA: No.

MAGDALENA: Come on!

MARTIRIO: I don't know what you're talking about!

MAGDALENA: Both of you know it better than I do, always with your heads together, like two little sheep, but not letting anybody else in on it. I mean about Pepe el Romano!

MARTIRIO: Ah!

MAGDALENA [*mocking her*]: Ah! The whole town's talking about it. Pepe el Romano is coming to marry Angustias. Last night he was walking around the house and I think he's going to send a declaration soon.

MARTIRIO: I'm glad. He's a good man.

AMELIA: Me too. Angustias is well off.

MAGDALENA: Neither one of you is glad.

MARTIRIO: Magdalena! What do you mean?

MAGDALENA: If he were coming because of Angustias' looks, for Angustias as a woman, I'd be glad too, but he's coming for her money. Even though Angustias is our sister, we're her family here and we know she's old and sickly, and always has been the least attractive one of us! Because if she looked like a dressed-up stick at twenty, what can she look like now, now that she's forty?

MARTIRIO: Don't talk like that. Luck comes to the one who least expects it.

AMELIA: But Magdalena's right after all! Angustias has all her father's money; she's the only rich one in the house and that's why, now that Father's dead and the money will be divided, they're coming for her.

MAGDALENA: Pepe el Romano is twenty-five years old and the best-looking man around here. The natural thing would be for him to be after you, Amelia, or our Adela, who's twenty – not looking for the least likely one in this house, a woman who, like her father, talks through her nose.

MARTIRIO: Maybe he likes that!

MAGDALENA: I've never been able to bear your hypocrisy.

MARTIRIO: Heavens!

[ADELA *enters*.]

MAGDALENA: Did the chickens see you?

ADELA: What did you want me to do?

AMELIA: If Mother sees you, she'll drag you by your hair!

ADELA: I had a lot of illusions about this dress. I'd planned to put it on the day we were going to eat water-melons at the well. There wouldn't have been another like it.

MARTIRIO: It's a lovely dress.

ADELA: And one that looks very good on me. It's the best thing Magdalena's ever cut.

MAGDALENA: And the chickens, what did they say to you?

ADELA: They presented me with a few fleas that riddled my legs.
 [*They laugh.*]

MARTIRIO: What you can do is dye it black.

MAGDALENA: The best thing you can do is give it to Angustias for her wedding with Pepe el Romano.

ADELA [*with hidden emotion*]: But Pepe el Romano . . .

AMELIA: Haven't you heard about it?

ADELA: No.

MAGDALENA: Well, now you know!

ADELA: But it can't be!

MAGDALENA: Money can do anything.

ADELA: Is that why she went out after the funeral and stood looking through the door?
 [*Pause.*]
 And that man would . . .

MAGDALENA: Would do anything.
 [*Pause.*]

MARTIRIO: What are you thinking, Adela?

ADELA: I'm thinking that this mourning has caught me at the worst moment of my life for me to bear it.

MAGDALENA: You'll get used to it.

ADELA [*bursting out, crying with rage*]: I will not get used to it! I can't be locked up. I don't want my skin to look like yours. I don't want my skin's whiteness lost in these rooms. Tomorrow I'm going to put on my green dress and go walking in the streets. I want to go out!

[*The* FIRST SERVANT *enters.*]

MAGDALENA [*in a tone of authority*]: Adela!

SERVANT: The poor thing! How she misses her father....

[*She goes out.*]

MARTIRIO: Hush!

AMELIA: What happens to one will happen to all of us.

[ADELA *grows calm.*]

MAGDALENA: The servant almost heard you.

SERVANT [*entering*]: Pepe el Romano is coming along at the end of the street.

[AMELIA, MARTIRIO, *and* MAGDALENA *run hurriedly.*]

MAGDALENA: Let's go see him!

[*They leave rapidly.*]

SERVANT [*to* ADELA]: Aren't you going?

ADELA: It's nothing to me.

SERVANT: Since he has to turn the corner, you'll see him better from the window of your room.

[*The* SERVANT *goes out.* ADELA *is left on the stage, standing doubtfully; after a moment, she also leaves rapidly, going toward her room.* BERNARDA *and* PONCIA *come in.*]

BERNARDA: Damned portions and shares.

PONCIA: What a lot of money is left to Angustias!

BERNARDA: Yes.

PONCIA: And for the others, considerably less.

BERNARDA: You've told me that three times now, when you know I don't want it mentioned! Considerably less; a lot less! Don't remind me any more.

[ANGUSTIAS *comes in, her face heavily made up.*]

Angustias!

ANGUSTIAS: Mother.

BERNARDA: Have you dared to powder your face? Have you dared to wash your face on the day of your father's death?

ANGUSTIAS: He wasn't my father. Mine died a long time ago. Have you forgotten that already?

BERNARDA: You owe more to this man, father of your sisters, than to your own. Thanks to him, your fortune is intact.

ANGUSTIAS: We'll have to see about that first!

BERNARDA: Even out of decency! Out of respect!

ANGUSTIAS: Let me go out, Mother!

BERNARDA: Let you go out? After I've taken that powder off your face, I will. Spineless! Painted hussy! Just like your aunts!

[*She removes the powder violently with her handkerchief.*]

Now get out!

PONCIA: Bernarda, don't be so hateful!

BERNARDA: Even though my mother is crazy, I still have my five senses and I know what I'm doing.

[*They all enter.*]

MAGDALENA: What's going on here?

BERNARDA: Nothing's 'going on here'!

MAGDALENA [*to* ANGUSTIAS]: If you're fighting over the inheritance you're the richest one and can hang on to it all.

ANGUSTIAS: Keep your tongue in your pocketbook!

BERNARDA [*beating on the floor*]: Don't fool yourselves into thinking you'll sway me. Until I go out of this house feet first I'll give the orders for myself and for you!

[*Voices are heard and* MARÍA JOSEFA, *Bernarda's mother, enters. She is very old and has decked out her head and breast with flowers.*]

MARÍA JOSEFA: Bernarda, where is my mantilla? Nothing, nothing of what I own will be for any of you. Not my rings nor my black moiré dress. Because not a one of you is going to marry – not a one. Bernarda, give me my necklace of pearls.

BERNARDA [*to the* SERVANT]: Why did you let her get in here?

SERVANT [*trembling*]: She got away from me!

MARÍA JOSEFA: I ran away because I want to marry – I want to get married to a beautiful manly man from the shore of the sea. Because here the men run from women.

BERNARDA: Hush, hush, Mother!

MARÍA JOSEFA: No, no – I won't hush. I don't want to see these single women, longing for marriage, turning their hearts to dust; and I want to go to my home town. Bernarda, I want a man to get married to and be happy with!

BERNARDA: Lock her up!

MARÍA JOSEFA: Let me go out, Bernarda!

[*The* SERVANT *seizes* MARÍA JOSEFA.]

BERNARDA: Help her, all of you!

[*They all grab the old woman.*]

MARÍA JOSEFA: I want to get away from here! Bernarda! To get married by the shore of the sea – by the shore of the sea!

QUICK CURTAIN

ACT TWO

A white room in BERNARDA'S *house. The doors on the left lead to the bedrooms.*

[BERNARDA'S DAUGHTERS *are seated on low chairs, sewing.* MAGDALENA *is embroidering.* PONCIA *is with them.*]

ANGUSTIAS: I've cut the third sheet.

MARTIRIO: That one goes to Amelia.

MAGDALENA: Angustias, shall I put Pepe's initials here too?

ANGUSTIAS [*dryly*]: No.

MAGDALENA [*calling from off stage to* ADELA]: Adela, aren't you coming?

AMELIA: She's probably stretched out on the bed.

PONCIA: Something's wrong with that one. I find her restless, trembling, frightened – as if a lizard were between her breasts.

MARTIRIO: There's nothing, more or less, wrong with her than there is with all of us.

MAGDALENA: All of us except Angustias.

ANGUSTIAS: I feel fine, and anybody who doesn't like it can pop.

MAGDALENA: We all have to admit the nicest things about you are your figure and your tact.

ANGUSTIAS: Fortunately, I'll soon be out of this hell.

MAGDALENA: Maybe you won't get out!

MARTIRIO: Stop this talk!

ANGUSTIAS: Besides, a good dowry is better than dark eyes in one's face!

MAGDALENA: All you say just goes in one ear and out the other.

AMELIA [*to* PONCIA]: Open the patio door and see if we can get a bit of a breeze.

[PONCIA *opens the door.*]

MARTIRIO: Last night I couldn't sleep because of the heat.

AMELIA: Neither could I.

MAGDALENA: I got up for a bit of air. There was a black storm-cloud and a few drops even fell.

PONCIA: It was one in the morning and the earth seemed to give off fire. I got up too. Angustias was still at the window with Pepe.

MAGDALENA [*with irony*]: That late! What time did he leave?

ANGUSTIAS: Why do you ask, if you saw him?

AMELIA: He must have left about one-thirty.

ANGUSTIAS: Yes. How did you know?

AMELIA: I heard him cough and heard his mare's hoof-beats.

PONCIA: But I heard him leave around four.

ANGUSTIAS: It must have been someone else!

PONCIA: No, I'm sure of it!

AMELIA: That's what it seemed to me, too.

MAGDALENA: That's very strange!

[*Pause.*]

PONCIA: Listen, Angustias, what did he say to you the first time he came by your window?

ANGUSTIAS: Nothing. What should he say? Just talked.

MARTIRIO: It's certainly strange that two people who never knew each other should suddenly meet at a window and be engaged.

ANGUSTIAS: Well, I didn't mind.

AMELIA: I'd have felt very strange about it.

ANGUSTIAS: No, because when a man comes to a window he knows, from all the busybodies who come and go and fetch and carry, that he's going to be told 'yes'.

MARTIRIO: All right, but he'd have to ask you.

ANGUSTIAS: Of course!

AMELIA [*inquisitively*]: And how did he ask you?

ANGUSTIAS: Why, no way: 'You know I'm after you. I need a good, well brought-up woman, and that's you – if it's agreeable.'

AMELIA: These things embarrass me!

ANGUSTIAS: They embarrass me too, but one has to go through it!

PONCIA: And did he say anything more?

ANGUSTIAS: Yes, he did all the talking.

MARTIRIO: And you?

ANGUSTIAS: I couldn't have said a word. My heart was almost coming out of my mouth. It was the first time I'd ever been alone at night with a man.

MAGDALENA: And such a handsome man.

ANGUSTIAS: He's not bad-looking!

PONCIA: Those things happen among people who have an idea how to do things, who talk and say and move their hand. The first time my husband, Evaristo the Short-tailed, came to my window . . . Ha! Ha! Ha!

AMELIA: What happened?

PONCIA: It was very dark. I saw him coming along and as he went by he said, 'Good evening.' 'Good evening,' I said. Then we were both silent for more than half an hour. The sweat poured down my body. Then Evaristo got nearer and nearer as if he wanted to squeeze in through the bars and said in a very low voice – 'Come here and let me feel you!'

[*They all laugh.* AMELIA *gets up, runs, and looks through the door.*]

AMELIA: Ay, I thought Mother was coming!

MAGDALENA: What she'd have done to us!

[*They go on laughing.*]

AMELIA: Sh-h-h! She'll hear us.

PONCIA: Then he acted very decently. Instead of getting some other idea, he went to raising birds, until he died. You aren't married but it's good for you to know, anyway, that two weeks after the wedding a man gives up the bed for the table, then the table for the tavern, and the woman who doesn't like it can just rot, weeping in a corner.

AMELIA: You liked it.

PONCIA: I learned how to handle him!

MARTIRIO: Is it true that you sometimes hit him?

PONCIA: Yes, and once I almost poked out one of his eyes!

MAGDALENA: All women ought to be like that!

PONCIA: I'm one of your mother's school. One time I don't know what he said to me, and then I killed all his birds – with the pestle!

[*They laugh.*]

MAGDALENA: Adela, child! Don't miss this.

AMELIA: Adela!

[*Pause.*]

MAGDALENA: I'll go see!

[*She goes out.*]

PONCIA: That child is sick!

MARTIRIO: Of course. She hardly sleeps!

PONCIA: What *does* she do, then?

MARTIRIO: How do I know what she does?

PONCIA: You probably know better than we do, since you sleep with just a wall between you.

ANGUSTIAS: Envy gnaws on people.

AMELIA: Don't exaggerate.

ANGUSTIAS: I can tell it in her eyes. She's getting the look of a crazy woman.

MARTIRIO: Don't talk about crazy women. This is one place you're not allowed to say that word.

[MAGDALENA *and* ADELA *enter.*]

MAGDALENA: Didn't you say she was asleep?

ADELA: My body aches.

MARTIRIO [*with a hidden meaning*]: Didn't you sleep well last night?

ADELA: Yes.

MARTIRIO: Then?

ADELA [*loudly*]: Leave me alone. Awake or asleep, it's no affair of yours. I'll do whatever I want to with my body.

MARTIRIO: I was just concerned about you!

ADELA: Concerned? – curious! Weren't you sewing? Well, continue! I wish I were invisible so I could pass through a room without being asked where I was going!

SERVANT [*entering*]: Bernarda is calling you. The man with the laces is here.

[*All but* ADELA *and* PONCIA *go out, and as* MARTIRIO *leaves, she looks fixedly at* ADELA.]

ADELA: Don't look at me like that! If you want, I'll give you my eyes, for they're younger, and my back to improve that hump you have, but look the other way when I go by.

PONCIA: Adela, she's your sister, and the one who most loves you besides!

ADELA: She follows me everywhere. Sometimes she looks in my room to see if I'm sleeping. She won't let me breathe, and always, 'Too bad about that face!' 'Too bad about that body! It's going to waste!' But I won't let that happen. My body will be for whomever I choose.

PONCIA [*insinuatingly, in a low voice*]: For Pepe el Romano, no?

ADELA [*frightened*]: What do you mean?

PONCIA: What I said, Adela!

ADELA: Shut up!

PONCIA [*loudly*]: Don't you think I've noticed?

ADELA: Lower your voice!

PONCIA: Then forget what you're thinking about!

ADELA: What do you know?

PONCIA: We old ones can see through walls. Where do you go when you get up at night?

ADELA: I wish you were blind!

PONCIA: But my head and hands are full of eyes, where something like this is concerned. I couldn't possibly guess your intentions. Why did you sit almost naked at your window, and with the light on and window open, when Pepe passed by the second night he came to talk with your sister?

ADELA: That's not true!

PONCIA: Don't be a child! Leave your sister alone. And if you like Pepe el Romano, keep it to yourself.

[ADELA *weeps*.]

Besides, who says you can't marry him? Your sister Angustias is sickly. She'll die with her first child. Narrow-waisted, old – and out of my experience I can tell you she'll die. Then Pepe will do what all widowers do in these parts: he'll marry the youngest and most beautiful, and that's you. Live on that hope, forget him, anything; but don't go against God's law.

ADELA: Hush!

PONCIA: I won't hush!

ADELA: Mind your own business. Snooper, traitor!

PONCIA: I'm going to stick to you like a shadow!

ADELA: Instead of cleaning the house and then going to bed and praying for the dead, you root around like an old sow about goings on between men and women – so you can drool over them.

PONCIA: I keep watch; so people won't spit when they pass our door.

ADELA: What a tremendous affection you've suddenly conceived for my sister.

PONCIA: I don't have any affection for any of you. I want to live in a decent house. I don't want to be dirtied in my old age!

ADELA: Save your advice. It's already too late. For I'd leap not over you, just a servant, but over my mother to put out this fire I feel in my legs and my mouth. What can you possibly say about me? That I lock myself in my room and will not open the door? That I don't sleep? I'm smarter than you! See if you can catch the hare with your hands.

PONCIA: Don't defy me, Adela, don't defy me! Because I can shout, light lamps, and make bells ring.

ADELA: Bring four thousand yellow flares and set them about the walls of the yard. No one can stop what has to happen.

PONCIA: You like him that much?

ADELA: That much! Looking in his eyes I seem to drink his blood in slowly.

PONCIA: I won't listen to you.

ADELA: Well, you'll have to! I've been afraid of you. But now I'm stronger than you!

[ANGUSTIAS enters.]

ANGUSTIAS: Always arguing!

PONCIA: Certainly. She insists that in all this heat I have to go bring her I don't know what from the store.

ANGUSTIAS: Did you buy me the bottle of perfume?

PONCIA: The most expensive one. And the face powder. I put them on the table in your room.

[ANGUSTIAS *goes out.*]

ADELA: And be quiet!

PONCIA: We'll see!

[MARTIRIO *and* AMELIA *enter.*]

MARTIRIO [*to* ADELA]: Did you see the laces?

AMELIA: Angustias', for her wedding sheets, are beautiful.

ADELA [*to* MARTIRIO, *who is carrying some lace*]: And these?

MARTIRIO: They're for me. For a nightgown.

ADELA [*with sarcasm*]: One needs a sense of humour around here!

MARTIRIO [*meaningfully*]: But only for me to look at. I don't have to exhibit myself before anybody.

PONCIA: No one ever sees us in our nightgowns.

MARTIRIO [*meaningfully, looking at* ADELA]: Sometimes they don't! But I love nice underwear. If I were rich, I'd have it made of Holland cloth. It's one of the few tastes I've left.

PONCIA: These laces are beautiful for babies' caps and christening gowns. I could never afford them for my own. Now let's see if Angustias will use them for hers. Once she starts having children, they'll keep her running night and day.

MAGDALENA: I don't intend to sew a stitch on them.

AMELIA: And much less bring up some stranger's children. Look how our neighbours across the road are – making sacrifices for four brats.

PONCIA: They're better off than you. There at least they laugh and you can hear them fight.

MARTIRIO: Well, you go work for them, then.

PONCIA: No, fate has sent me to this nunnery!

[*Tiny bells are heard distantly as though through several thicknesses of wall.*]

MAGDALENA: It's the men going back to work.

PONCIA: It was three o'clock a minute ago.

MARTIRIO: With this sun!

ADELA [*sitting down*]: Ay! If only we could go out in the fields too!

MAGDALENA [*sitting down*]: Each class does what it has to!

MARTIRIO [*sitting down*]: That's it!

AMELIA [*sitting down*]: Ay!

PONCIA: There's no happiness like that in the fields right at this time of year. Yesterday morning the reapers arrived. Forty or fifty handsome young men.

MAGDALENA: Where are they from this year?

PONCIA: From far, far away. They came from the mountains! Happy! Like weathered trees! Shouting and throwing stones! Last night a woman who dresses in sequins and dances, with an accordion, arrived, and fifteen of them made a deal with her to take her to the olive grove. I saw them from far away. The one who talked with her was a boy with green eyes – tight knit as a sheaf of wheat.

AMELIA: Really?

ADELA: Are you sure?

PONCIA: Years ago another one of those women came here, and I myself gave my eldest son some money so he could go. Men need things like that.

ADELA: Everything's forgiven *them*.

AMELIA: To be born a woman's the worst possible punishment.

MAGDALENA: Even our eyes aren't our own.

[*A distant song is heard, coming nearer.*]

PONCIA: There they are. They have a beautiful song.

AMELIA: They're going out to reap now.

CHORUS:

> The reapers have set out
> Looking for ripe wheat;
> They'll carry off the hearts
> Of any girls they meet.

[*Tambourines and carrañacas are heard. Pause. They all listen in the silence cut by the sun.*]

AMELIA: And they don't mind the sun!

MARTIRIO: They reap through flames.

ADELA: How I'd like to be a reaper so I could come and go as I pleased. Then we could forget what's eating us all.

MARTIRIO: What do you have to forget?

ADELA: Each one of us has something.

MARTIRIO [*intensely*]: Each one!

PONCIA: Quiet! Quiet!

CHORUS [*very distantly*]:

> Throw wide your doors and windows,
> You girls who live in the town
> The reaper asks you for roses
> With which to deck his crown.

PONCIA: What a song!

MARTIRIO [*with nostalgia*]:

> Throw wide your doors and windows,
> You girls who live in the town

ADELA [*passionately*]:

> The reaper asks you for roses
> With which to deck his crown.

[*The song grows more distant.*]

PONCIA: Now they're turning the corner.

ADELA: Let's watch them from the window of my room.

PONCIA: Be careful not to open the shutter too much because they're likely to give them a push to see who's looking.

[*The three leave.* MARTIRIO *is left sitting on the low chair with her head between her hands.*]

AMELIA [*drawing near her*]: What's wrong with you?

MARTIRIO: The heat makes me feel ill.

AMELIA: And it's no more than that?

MARTIRIO: I was wishing it were November, the rainy days, the frost – anything except this unending summertime.

AMELIA: It'll pass and come again.

MARTIRIO: Naturally.

[*Pause.*]

What time did you go to sleep last night?

AMELIA: I don't know. I sleep like a log. Why?

MARTIRIO: Nothing. Only I thought I heard someone in the yard.

AMELIA: Yes?

MARTIRIO: Very late.

AMELIA: And weren't you afraid?

MARTIRIO: No. I've heard it other nights.

AMELIA: We'd better watch out! Couldn't it have been the shepherds?

MARTIRIO: The shepherds came at six.

AMELIA: Maybe a young, unbroken mule?

MARTIRIO [to herself, with double meaning]: That's it! That's it! An unbroken little mule.

AMELIA: We'll have to set a watch.

MARTIRIO: No. No. Don't say anything. It may be I've just imagined it.

AMELIA: Maybe.

[Pause. AMELIA starts to go.]

MARTIRIO: Amelia!

AMELIA [at the door]: What?

[Pause.]

MARTIRIO: Nothing.

[Pause.]

AMELIA: Why did you call me?

[Pause.]

MARTIRIO: It just came out. I didn't mean to.

[Pause.]

AMELIA: Lie down for a little.

ANGUSTIAS [she bursts in furiously, in a manner that makes a great contrast with previous silence]: Where's that picture of Pepe I had under my pillow? Which one of you has it?

MARTIRIO: No one.

AMELIA: You'd think he was a silver St Bartholomew.

ANGUSTIAS: Where's the picture?

[PONCIA, MAGDALENA, and ADELA enter.]

ADELA: What picture?

ANGUSTIAS: One of you has hidden it from me.

MAGDALENA: Do you have the effrontery to say that?

ANGUSTIAS: I had it in my room, and now it isn't there.

MARTIRIO: But couldn't it have jumped out into the yard at midnight? Pepe likes to walk around in the moonlight.

ANGUSTIAS: Don't joke with me! When he comes I'll tell him.

PONCIA: Don't do that! Because it'll turn up.

[*Looking at* ADELA]

ANGUSTIAS: I'd like to know which one of you has it.

ADELA [*looking at* MARTIRIO]: Somebody had it! But not me!

MARTIRIO [*with meaning*]: Of course not you!

BERNARDA [*entering with her cane*]: What scandal is this in my house in the heat's heavy silence? The neighbours must have their ears glued to the walls.

ANGUSTIAS: They've stolen my sweetheart's picture!

BERNARDA [*fiercely*]: Who? Who?

ANGUSTIAS: They have!

BERNARDA: Which one of you?

[*Silence.*]

Answer me!

[*Silence. To* PONCIA]

Search their rooms! Look in their beds. This comes of not tying you up with shorter leashes. But I'll teach you now!

[*To* ANGUSTIAS]

Are you sure?

ANGUSTIAS: Yes.

BERNARDA: Did you look everywhere?

ANGUSTIAS: Yes, Mother.

[*They all stand in an embarrassed silence.*]

BERNARDA: At the end of my life – to make me drink the bitterest poison a mother knows.

[*To* PONCIA]

Did you find it?

PONCIA: Here it is.

BERNARDA: Where did you find it?

PONCIA: It was . . .

BERNARDA: Say it! Don't be afraid.

PONCIA [*wonderingly*]: Between the sheets in Martirio's bed.

BERNARDA [*to* MARTIRIO]: Is that true?

MARTIRIO: It's true.

BERNARDA [*advancing on her, beating her with her cane*]: You'll come to a bad end yet, you hypocrite! Trouble-maker!

MARTIRIO [*fiercely*]: Don't hit me, Mother!

BERNARDA: All I want to!

MARTIRIO: If I let you! You hear me? Get back!

PONCIA: Don't be disrespectful to your mother!

ANGUSTIAS [*holding* BERNARDA]: Let her go, please!

BERNARDA: Not even tears in your eyes.

MARTIRIO: I'm not going to cry just to please you.

BERNARDA: Why did you take the picture?

MARTIRIO: Can't I play a joke on my sister? What else would I want it for?

ADELA [*leaping forward, full of jealousy*]: It wasn't a joke! You never liked to play jokes. It was something else bursting in her breast – trying to come out. Admit it openly now.

MARTIRIO: Hush, and don't make me speak; for if I should speak the walls would close together one against the other with shame.

ADELA: An evil tongue never stops inventing lies.

BERNARDA: Adela!

MAGDALENA: You're crazy.

AMELIA: And you stone us all with your evil suspicions.

MARTIRIO: But some others do things more wicked!

ADELA: Until all at once they stand forth stark naked and the river carries them along.

BERNARDA: Spiteful!

ANGUSTIAS: It's not my fault Pepe el Romano chose me!

ADELA: For your money.

ANGUSTIAS: Mother!

BERNARDA: Silence!

MARTIRIO: For your fields and your orchards.

MAGDALENA: That's only fair.

BERNARDA: Silence, I say! I saw the storm coming but I didn't think it'd burst so soon. Oh, what an avalanche of hate you've thrown on my heart! But I'm not old yet – I have five chains for you, and this house my father built, so not even the weeds will know of my desolation. Out of here!

[*They go out.* BERNARDA *sits down desolately.* PONCIA *is standing close to the wall.* BERNARDA *recovers herself, and beats on the floor.*]

I'll have to let them feel the weight of my hand! Bernarda, remember your duty!

PONCIA: May I speak?

BERNARDA: Speak. I'm sorry you heard. A stranger is always out of place in a family.

PONCIA: What I've seen, I've seen.

BERNARDA: Angustias must get married right away.

PONCIA: Certainly. We'll have to get her away from here.

BERNARDA: Not her, him!

PONCIA: Of course. He's the one to get away from here. You've thought it all out.

BERNARDA: I'm not thinking. There are things that shouldn't and can't be thought out. I give orders.

PONCIA: And you think he'll be satisfied to go away?

BERNARDA [*rising*]: What are you imagining now?

PONCIA: He will, of course, marry Angustias.

BERNARDA: Speak up! I know you well enough to see that your knife's out for me.

PONCIA: I never knew a warning could be called murder.

BERNARDA: Have you some 'warning' for me?

PONCIA: I'm not making any accusations, Bernarda. I'm only telling you to open your eyes and you'll see.

BERNARDA: See what?

PONCIA: You've always been smart, Bernarda. You've seen other people's sins a hundred miles away. Many times I've thought you could read minds. But, your children are your children, and now you're blind.

BERNARDA: Are you talking about Martirio?

PONCIA: Well, yes – about Martirio . . .

[*With curiosity*]

I wonder why she hid the picture?

BERNARDA [*shielding her daughter*]: After all, she says it was a joke. What else could it be?

PONCIA [*scornfully*]: Do you believe that?

BERNARDA [*sternly*]: I don't merely believe it. It's so!

PONCIA: Enough of this. We're talking about your family. But if we were talking about your neighbour across the way, what would it be?

BERNARDA: Now you're beginning to pull the point of the knife out.

PONCIA [*always cruelly*]: No, Bernarda. Something very grave is happening here. I don't want to put the blame on your shoulders, but you've never given your daughters any freedom. Martirio is lovesick, I don't care what you say. Why didn't you let her marry Enrique Humanas? Why, on the very day he was coming to her window, did you send him a message not to come?

BERNARDA [*loudly*]: I'd do it a thousand times over! My blood won't mingle with the Humanas' while I live! His father was a shepherd.

PONCIA: And you see now what's happening to you with these airs!

BERNARDA: I have them because I can afford to. And you don't have them because you know where you came from!

PONCIA [*with hate*]: Don't remind me! I'm old now. I've always been grateful for your protection.

BERNARDA [*emboldened*]: You don't seem so!

PONCIA [*with hate, behind softness*]: Martirio will forget this.

BERNARDA: And if she doesn't – the worse for her. I don't believe this is that 'very grave thing' that's happening here. Nothing's happening here. It's just that you wish it would! And if it should happen one day, you can be sure it won't go beyond these walls.

PONCIA: I'm not so sure of that! There are people in town who can also read hidden thoughts, from afar.

BERNARDA: How you'd like to see me and my daughters on our way to a whorehouse!

PONCIA: No one knows her own destiny!

BERNARDA: I know my destiny! And my daughters! The whorehouse was for a certain woman, already dead. . . .

PONCIA [*fiercely*]: Bernarda, respect the memory of my mother!

BERNARDA: Then don't plague me with your evil thoughts!
[*Pause.*]

PONCIA: I'd better stay out of everything.

BERNARDA: That's what you ought to do. Work and keep your mouth shut. The duty of all who work for a living.

PONCIA: But we can't do that. Don't you think it'd be better for Pepe to marry Martirio or . . . yes! . . . Adela?

BERNARDA: No, I *don't* think so.

PONCIA [*with meaning*]: Adela! She's Romano's real sweetheart!

BERNARDA: Things are never the way we want them!

PONCIA: But it's hard work to turn them from their destined course. For Pepe to be with Angustias seems wrong to me – and to other people – and even to the wind. Who knows if they'll get what they want?

BERNARDA: There you go again! Sneaking up on me – giving me bad dreams. But I won't listen to you, because if all you say should come to pass – I'd scratch your face.

PONCIA: Frighten someone else with that.

BERNARDA: Fortunately, my daughters respect me and have never gone against my will!

PONCIA: That's right! But as soon as they break loose they'll fly to the rooftops!

BERNARDA: And I'll bring them down with stones!

PONCIA: Oh yes! You were always the bravest one!

BERNARDA: I've always enjoyed a good fight!

PONCIA: But aren't people strange? You should see Angustias' enthusiasm for her lover, at her age! And he seems very smitten too. Yesterday my oldest son told me that when he passed by with the oxen at four-thirty in the morning they were still talking.

BERNARDA: At four-thirty?

ANGUSTIAS [*entering*]: That's a lie!

PONCIA: That's what he told me.

BERNARDA [*to* ANGUSTIAS]: Speak up!

ANGUSTIAS: For more than a week Pepe has been leaving at one. May God strike me dead if I'm lying.

MARTIRIO [*entering*]: I heard him leave at four too.

BERNARDA: But did you see him with your eyes?

MARTIRIO: I didn't want to look out. Don't you talk now through the side windows?

ANGUSTIAS: We talk through my bedroom window.

[ADELA *appears at the door.*]

MARTIRIO: Then . . .

BERNARDA: What's going on here?

PONCIA: If you're not careful, you'll find out! At least Pepe was at *one* of your windows – and at four in the morning too!

BERNARDA: Are you sure of that?

PONCIA: You can't be sure of anything in this life!

ADELA: Mother, don't listen to someone who wants us to lose everything we have.

BERNARDA: I know how to take care of myself! If the townspeople want to come bearing false witness against me, they'll run into a stone wall! Don't any of you talk about this! Sometimes other people try to stir up a wave of filth to drown us.

MARTIRIO: I don't like to lie.

PONCIA: So there must be something.

BERNARDA: There won't be anything. I was born to have my eyes always open. Now I'll watch without closing them till I die.

ANGUSTIAS: I have the right to know.

BERNARDA: You don't have any right except to obey. No one's going to fetch and carry for me.

[*To* PONCIA]

And don't meddle in our affairs. No one will take a step without my knowing it.

SERVANT [*entering*]: There's a big crowd at the top of the street, and all the neighbours are at their doors!

BERNARDA [*to* PONCIA]: Run, see what's happening!

[*The* GIRLS *are about to run out.*]

Where are you going? I always knew you for window-watching
women and breakers of your mourning. All of you, to the patio!

[*They go out.* BERNARDA *leaves. Distant shouts are heard.* MAR-
TIRIO *and* ADELA *enter and listen, not daring to step farther than the
front door.*]

MARTIRIO: You can be thankful I didn't happen to open my mouth.

ADELA: I would have spoken too.

MARTIRIO: And what were you going to say? Wanting isn't doing!

ADELA: I do what I can and what happens to suit me. You've wanted
to, but haven't been able.

MARTIRIO: You won't go on very long.

ADELA: I'll have everything!

MARTIRIO: I'll tear you out of his arms!

ADELA [*pleadingly*]: Martirio, let me be!

MARTIRIO: None of us will have him!

ADELA: He wants me for his house!

MARTIRIO: I saw how he embraced you!

ADELA: I didn't want him to. It's as if I were dragged by a rope.

MARTIRIO: I'll see you dead first!

[MAGDALENA *and* ANGUSTIAS *look in. The tumult is increasing.*
A SERVANT *enters with* BERNARDA. PONCIA *also enters from an-*
other room.]

PONCIA: Bernarda!

BERNARDA: What's happening?

PONCIA: Librada's daughter, the unmarried one, had a child and no
one knows whose it is!

ADELA: A child?

PONCIA: And to hide her shame she killed it and hid it under the
rocks, but the dogs, with more heart than most Christians, dug
it out and, as though directed by the hand of God, left it at her
door. Now they want to kill her. They're dragging her through
the streets – and down the paths and across the olive groves the
men are coming, shouting so the fields shake.

BERNARDA: Yes, let them all come with olive whips and hoe handles
– let them all come and kill her!

ADELA: No, not to kill her!

MARTIRIO: Yes – and let us go out too!

BERNARDA: And whoever loses her decency pay for it!

[*Outside a woman's shriek and a great clamour is heard.*]

ADELA: Let her escape! Don't you go out!

MARTIRIO [*looking at* ADELA]: Let her pay what she owes!

BERNARDA [*at the archway*]: Finish her before the guards come! Hot coals in the place where she sinned!

ADELA [*holding her belly*]: No! No!

BERNARDA: Kill her! Kill her!

CURTAIN

ACT THREE

Four white walls, lightly washed in blue, of the interior patio of BERNARDA
ALBA's *house. The doorways, illumined by the lights inside the rooms, give
a tenuous glow to the stage.*

[*At the centre there is a table with a shaded oil-lamp about which*
BERNARDA *and her* DAUGHTERS *are eating.* LA PONCIA *serves
them.* PRUDENCIA *sits apart. When the curtain rises, there is a great
silence interrupted only by the noise of plates and silverware.*]

PRUDENCIA: I'm going. I've made you a long visit.

[*She rises.*]

BERNARDA: But wait, Prudencia. We never see one another.

PRUDENCIA: Have they sounded the last call to rosary?

PONCIA: Not yet.

[PRUDENCIA *sits down again.*]

BERNARDA: And your husband, how's he getting on?

PRUDENCIA: The same.

BERNARDA: We never see him either.

PRUDENCIA: You know how he is. Since he quarrelled with his
brothers over the inheritance, he hasn't used the front door. He
takes a ladder and climbs over the back wall.

BERNARDA: He's a real man! And your daughter?

PRUDENCIA: He's never forgiven her.

BERNARDA: He's right.

PRUDENCIA: I don't know what he told you. I suffer because
of it.

BERNARDA: A daughter who's disobedient stops being a daughter
and becomes an enemy.

PRUDENCIA: I let water run. The only consolation I've left is to take
refuge in the church, but, since I'm losing my sight, I'll have to stop
coming so the children won't make fun of me.

[*A heavy blow is heard against the walls.*]

What's that?

BERNARDA: The stallion. He's locked in the stall and he kicks against the wall of the house.

[*Shouting*]

Tether him and take him out in the yard!

[*In a lower voice*]

He must be too hot.

PRUDENCIA: Are you going to put the new mares to him?

BERNARDA: At daybreak.

PRUDENCIA: You've known how to increase your stock.

BERNARDA: By dint of money and struggling.

PONCIA [*interrupting*]: And she has the best herd in these parts. It's a shame that prices are low.

BERNARDA: Do you want a little cheese and honey?

PRUDENCIA: I have no appetite.

[*The blow is heard again.*]

PONCIA: My God!

PRUDENCIA: It quivered in my chest!

BERNARDA [*rising, furiously*]: Do I have to say things twice? Let him out to roll on the straw.

[*Pause. Then, as though speaking to the Stableman*]

Well then, lock the mares in the corral, but let him run free or he may kick down the walls.

[*She returns to the table and sits again.*]

Ay, what a life!

PRUDENCIA: You have to fight like a man.

BERNARDA: That's it.

[ADELA *gets up from the table.*]

Where are you going?

ADELA: For a drink of water.

BERNARDA [*raising her voice*]: Bring a pitcher of cool water.

[*To* ADELA]

You can sit down.

[ADELA *sits down.*]

PRUDENCIA: And Angustias, when will she get married?

BERNARDA: They're coming to ask for her within three days.

PRUDENCIA: You must be happy.

ANGUSTIAS: Naturally!

AMELIA [*to* MAGDALENA]: You've spilled the salt!

MAGDALENA: You can't possibly have worse luck than you're having.

AMELIA: It always brings bad luck.

BERNARDA: That's enough!

PRUDENCIA [*to* ANGUSTIAS]: Has he given you the ring yet?

ANGUSTIAS: Look at it.

    [*She holds it out.*]

PRUDENCIA: It's beautiful. Three pearls. In my day, pearls signified tears.

ANGUSTIAS: But things have changed now.

ADELA: I don't think so. Things go on meaning the same. Engagement rings should be diamonds.

PONCIA: The most appropriate.

BERNARDA: With pearls or without them, things are as one proposes.

MARTIRIO: Or as God disposes.

PRUDENCIA: I've been told your furniture is beautiful.

BERNARDA: It cost sixteen thousand *reales*.

PONCIA [*interrupting*]: The best is the wardrobe with the mirror.

PRUDENCIA: I never saw a piece like that.

BERNARDA: We had chests.

PRUDENCIA: The important thing is that everything be for the best.

ADELA: And that you never know.

BERNARDA: There's no reason why it shouldn't be.

    [*Bells are heard very distantly.*]

PRUDENCIA: The last call.

    [*To* ANGUSTIAS]

  I'll be coming back to have you show me your clothes.

ANGUSTIAS: Whenever you like.

PRUDENCIA: Good evening – God bless you!

BERNARDA: Good-bye, Prudencia.

ALL FIVE DAUGHTERS [*at the same time*]: God go with you!

    [*Pause.* PRUDENCIA *goes out.*]

BERNARDA: Well, we've eaten.

[*They rise.*]

ADELA: I'm going to walk as far as the gate to stretch my legs and get a bit of fresh air.

[MAGDALENA *sits down in a low chair and leans against the wall.*]

AMELIA: I'll go with you.

MARTIRIO: I too.

ADELA [*with contained hate*]: I'm not going to get lost!

AMELIA: One needs company at night.

[*They go out.* BERNARDA *sits down.* ANGUSTIAS *is clearing the table.*]

BERNARDA: I've told you once already! I want you to talk to your sister Martirio. What happened about the picture was a joke and you must forget it.

ANGUSTIAS: You know she doesn't like me.

BERNARDA: Each one knows what she thinks inside. I don't pry into anyone's heart, but I want to put up a good front and have family harmony. You understand?

ANGUSTIAS: Yes.

BERNARDA: Then that's settled.

MAGDALENA [*she is almost asleep*]: Besides, you'll be gone in no time.

[*She falls asleep.*]

ANGUSTIAS: Not soon enough for me.

BERNARDA: What time did you stop talking last night?

ANGUSTIAS: Twelve-thirty.

BERNARDA: What does Pepe talk about?

ANGUSTIAS: I find him absent-minded. He always talks to me as though he were thinking of something else. If I ask him what's the matter, he answers: 'We men have our worries.'

BERNARDA: You shouldn't ask him. And when you're married, even less. Speak if he speaks, and look at him when he looks at you. That way you'll get along.

ANGUSTIAS: But, Mother, I think he's hiding things from me.

BERNARDA: Don't try to find out. Don't ask him, and above all, never let him see you cry.

ANGUSTIAS: I should be happy, but I'm not.

BERNARDA: It's all the same.

ANGUSTIAS: Many nights I watch Pepe very closely through the window bars and he seems to fade away – as though he were hidden in a cloud of dust like those raised by the flocks.

BERNARDA: That's just because you're not strong.

ANGUSTIAS: I hope so!

BERNARDA: Is he coming tonight?

ANGUSTIAS: No, he went into town with his mother.

BERNARDA: Good, we'll get to bed early. Magdalena!

ANGUSTIAS: She's asleep.

[ADELA, MARTIRIO, *and* AMELIA *enter.*]

AMELIA: What a dark night!

ADELA: You can't see two steps in front of you.

MARTIRIO: A good night for robbers, for anyone who needs to hide.

ADELA: The stallion was in the middle of the corral. White. Twice as large. Filling all the darkness.

AMELIA: It's true. It was frightening. Like a ghost.

ADELA: The sky has stars as big as fists.

MARTIRIO: This one stared at them till she almost cracked her neck.

ADELA: Don't you like them up there?

MARTIRIO: What goes on over the roof doesn't mean a thing to me. I have my hands full with what happens under it.

ADELA: Well, that's the way it goes with you!

BERNARDA: And it goes the same for you as for her.

ANGUSTIAS: Good night.

ADELA: Are you going to bed now?

ANGUSTIAS: Yes, Pepe isn't coming tonight.

[*She goes out.*]

ADELA: Mother, why, when a star falls or lightning flashes, does one say:

> Holy Barbara, blessed on high
> May your name be in the sky
> With holy water written high?

BERNARDA: The old people know many things we've forgotten.

AMELIA: I close my eyes so I won't see them.

ADELA: Not I. I like to see what's quiet and been quiet for years on end, running with fire.

MARTIRIO: But all that has nothing to do with us.

BERNARDA: And it's better not to think about it.

ADELA: What a beautiful night! I'd like to stay up till very late and enjoy the breeze from the fields.

BERNARDA: But we have to go to bed. Magdalena!

AMELIA: She's just dropped off.

BERNARDA: Magdalena!

MAGDALENA [*annoyed*]: Leave me alone!

BERNARDA: To bed!

MAGDALENA [*rising, in a bad humour*]: You don't give anyone a moment's peace!

[*She goes off grumbling.*]

AMELIA: Good night!

[*She goes out.*]

BERNARDA: You two get along, too.

MARTIRIO: How is it Angustias' sweetheart isn't coming tonight?

BERNARDA: He went on a trip.

MARTIRIO [*looking at* ADELA]: Ah!

ADELA: I'll see you in the morning!

[*She goes out.* MARTIRIO *drinks some water and goes out slowly, looking at the door to the yard.* PONCIA *enters.*]

PONCIA: Are you still here?

BERNARDA: Enjoying this quiet and not seeing anywhere the 'very grave thing' that's happening here – according to you.

PONCIA: Bernarda, let's not go any further with this.

BERNARDA: In this house there's no question of a yes or a no. My watchfulness can take care of anything.

PONCIA: Nothing's happening outside. That's true, all right. Your daughters act and are as though stuck in a cupboard. But neither you nor anyone else can keep watch inside a person's heart.

BERNARDA: My daughters breathe calmly enough.

PONCIA: That's your business, since you're their mother. I have enough to do just with serving you.

BERNARDA: Yes, you've turned quiet now.

PONCIA: I keep my place – that's all.

BERNARDA: The trouble is you've nothing to talk about. If there were grass in this house, you'd make it your business to put the neighbours' sheep to pasture here.

PONCIA: I hide more than you think.

BERNARDA: Do your sons still see Pepe at four in the morning? Are they still repeating this house's evil litany?

PONCIA: They say nothing.

BERNARDA: Because they can't. Because there's nothing for them to sink their teeth in. And all because my eyes keep constant watch!

PONCIA: Bernarda, I don't want to talk about this because I'm afraid of what you'll do. But don't you feel so safe.

BERNARDA: Very safe!

PONCIA: Who knows, lightning might strike suddenly. Who knows but what all of a sudden, in a rush of blood, your heart might stop.

BERNARDA: Nothing will happen here. I'm on guard now against all your suspicions.

PONCIA: All the better for you.

BERNARDA: Certainly, all the better!

SERVANT [entering]: I've just finished with the dishes. Is there anything else, Bernarda?

BERNARDA [rising]: Nothing. I'm going to get some rest.

PONCIA: What time do you want me to call you?

BERNARDA: No time. Tonight I intend to sleep well.

[She goes out.]

PONCIA: When you're powerless against the sea, it's easier to turn your back on it and not look at it.

SERVANT: She's so proud! She herself pulls the blindfold over her eyes.

PONCIA: I can do nothing. I tried to head things off, but now they frighten me too much. You feel this silence? – in each room there's a thunderstorm – and the day it breaks, it'll sweep all of us along with it. But I've said what I had to say.

SERVANT: Bernarda thinks nothing can stand against her, yet she doesn't know the strength a man has among women alone.

PONCIA: It's not all the fault of Pepe el Romano. It's true last year he was running after Adela; and she was crazy about him – but she ought to keep her place and not lead him on. A man's a man.

SERVANT: And some there are who believe he didn't have to talk many times with Adela.

PONCIA: That's true.

[*In a low voice*]

And some other things.

SERVANT: I don't know what's going to happen here.

PONCIA: How I'd like to sail across the sea and leave this house, this battleground, behind!

SERVANT: Bernarda's hurrying the wedding and it's possible nothing will happen.

PONCIA: Things have gone much too far already. Adela is set no matter what comes, and the rest of them watch without rest.

SERVANT: Martirio too . . . ?

PONCIA: That one's the worst. She's a pool of poison. She sees El Romano is not for her, and she'd sink the world if it were in her hand to do so.

SERVANT: How bad they all are!

PONCIA: They're women without men, that's all. And in such matters even blood is forgotten. Sh-h-h-h!

[*She listens.*]

SERVANT: What's the matter?

PONCIA [*she rises*]: The dogs are barking.

SERVANT: Someone must have passed by the back door

[ADELA *enters wearing a white petticoat and corselet.*]

PONCIA: Aren't you in bed yet?

ADELA: I want a drink of water.

[*She drinks from a glass on the table.*]

PONCIA: I imagined you were asleep.

ADELA: I got thirsty and woke up. Aren't you two going to get some rest?

SERVANT: Soon now.

[ADELA *goes out.*]

PONCIA: Let's go.

SERVANT: We've certainly earned some sleep. Bernarda doesn't let me rest the whole day.

PONCIA: Take the light.

SERVANT: The dogs are going mad.

PONCIA: They're not going to let us sleep.

[*They go out. The stage is left almost dark.* MARÍA JOSEFA *enter with a lamb in her arms.*]

MARÍA JOSEFA [*singing*]:

> Little lamb, child of mine,
> Let's go to the shore of the sea,
> The tiny ant will be at his doorway,
> I'll nurse you and give you your bread.
> Bernarda, old leopard-face,
> And Magdalena, hyena-face,
> Little lamb . . .
> Rock, rock-a-bye,
> Let's go to the palms at Bethlehem's gate.

[*She laughs.*]

> Neither you nor I would want to sleep
> The door will open by itself
> And on the beach we'll go and hide
> In a little coral cabin.
> Bernarda, old leopard-face,
> And Magdalena, hyena-face,
> Little lamb . . .
> Rock, rock-a-bye,
> Let's go to the palms at Bethlehem's gate.

[*She goes off singing.*]

[ADELA *enters. She looks about cautiously and disappears out the door leading to the corral.* MARTIRIO *enters by another door and stands in anguished watchfulness near the centre of the stage. She also is in petti-coats. She covers herself with a small black scarf.* MARÍA JOSEFA *crosses before her.*]

MARTIRIO: Grandmother, where are you going?

MARÍA JOSEFA: You are going to open the door for me? Who are you?

MARTIRIO: How did you get out here?

MARÍA JOSEFA: I escaped. You, who are you?

MARTIRIO: Go back to bed.

MARÍA JOSEFA: You're Martirio. Now I see you. Martirio, face of a martyr. And when are you going to have a baby? I've had this one.

MARTIRIO: Where did you get that lamb?

MARÍA JOSEFA: I know it's a lamb. But can't a lamb be a baby? It's better to have a lamb than not to have anything. Old Bernarda, leopard-face, and Magdalena, hyena-face!

MARTIRIO: Don't shout.

MARÍA JOSEFA: It's true. Everything's very dark. Just because I have white hair you think I can't have babies, but I can – babies and babies and babies. This baby will have white hair, and I'll have *this* baby, and another, and this *one* other; and with all of us with snow-white hair we'll be like the waves – one, then another, and another. Then we'll all sit down and all of us will have white heads, and we'll be seafoam. Why isn't there any seafoam here? Nothing but mourning shrouds here.

MARTIRIO: Hush, hush.

MARÍA JOSEFA: When my neighbour had a baby, I'd carry her some chocolate and later she'd bring me some, and so on – always and always and always. You'll have white hair, but your neighbours won't come. Now I have to go away, but I'm afraid the dogs will bite me. Won't you come with me as far as the fields? I don't like fields. I like houses, but open houses, and the neighbour women asleep in their beds with their little tiny tots, and the men outside sitting in their chairs. Pepe el Romano is a giant. All of you love him. But he's going to devour you because you're grains of wheat. No, not grains of wheat. Frogs with no tongues!

MARTIRIO [*angrily*]: Come, off to bed with you.

[*She pushes her.*]

MARÍA JOSEFA: Yes, but then you'll open the door for me, won't you?

MARTIRIO: Of course.

MARÍA JOSEFA [*weeping*]:

Little lamb, child of mine.
Let's go to the shore of the sea,
The tiny ant will be at his doorway,
I'll nurse you and give you your bread.

[MARTIRIO *locks the door through which* MARÍA JOSEFA *came out and goes to the yard door. There she hesitates, but goes two steps farther.*]

MARTIRIO [*in a low voice*]: Adela!

[*Pause. She advances to the door. Then, calling*]

Adela!

[ADELA *enters. Her hair is disarranged.*]

ADELA: And what are you looking for me for?

MARTIRIO: Keep away from him.

ADELA: Who are you to tell me that?

MARTIRIO: That's no place for a decent woman.

ADELA: How you wish *you'd* been there!

MARTIRIO [*shouting*]: This is the moment for me to speak. This can't go on.

ADELA: This is just the beginning. I've had strength enough to push myself forward – the spirit and looks you lack. I've seen death under this roof, and gone out to look for what was mine, what belonged to me.

MARTIRIO: That soulless man came for another woman. You pushed yourself in front of him.

ADELA: He came for the money, but his eyes were always on me.

MARTIRIO: I won't allow you to snatch him away. He'll marry Angustias.

ADELA: You know better than I he doesn't love her.

MARTIRIO: I know.

ADELA: You know because you've seen – he loves me, me!

MARTIRIO [*desperately*]: Yes.

ADELA [*close before her*]: He loves me, *me*! He loves me, *me*!

MARTIRIO: Stick me with a knife if you like, but don't tell me that again.

ADELA: That's why you're trying to fix it so I won't go away with him. It makes no difference to you if he puts his arms around a woman he doesn't love. Nor does it to me. He could be a hundred years with Angustias, but for him to have his arms around me seems terrible to you – because you too love him! You love him!

MARTIRIO [*dramatically*]: Yes! Let me say it without hiding my head. Yes! My breast's bitter, bursting like a pomegranate. I love him!

ADELA [*impulsively, hugging her*]: Martirio, Martirio, I'm not to blame!

MARTIRIO: Don't put your arms around me! Don't try to smooth it over. My blood's no longer yours, and even though I try to think of you as a sister, I see you as just another woman.

[*She pushes her away.*]

ADELA: There's no way out here. Whoever has to drown – let her drown. Pepe is mine. He'll carry me to the rushes along the river-bank . . .

MARTIRIO: He won't!

ADELA: I can't stand this horrible house after the taste of his mouth. I'll be what he wants me to be. Everybody in the village against me, burning me with their fiery fingers; pursued by those who claim they're decent, and I'll wear, before them all, the crown of thorns that belongs to the mistress of a married man.

MARTIRIO: Hush!

ADELA: Yes, yes.

[*In a low voice*]

Let's go to bed. Let's let him marry Angustias. I don't care any more, but I'll go off alone to a little house where he'll come to see me whenever he wants, whenever he feels like it.

MARTIRIO: That'll never happen! Not while I have a drop of blood left in my body.

ADELA: Not just weak you, but a wild horse I could force to his knees with just the strength of my little finger.

MARTIRIO: Don't raise that voice of yours to me. It irritates me. I have a heart full of a force so evil that, without my wanting to be, I'm drowned by it.

ADELA: You show us the way to love our sisters. God must have meant to leave me alone in the midst of darkness, because I can see you as I've never seen you before.

[*A whistle is heard and* ADELA *runs toward the door, but* MARTIRIO *gets in front of her.*]

MARTIRIO: Where are you going?

ADELA: Get away from that door!

MARTIRIO: Get by me if you can!

ADELA: Get away!

[*They struggle.*]

MARTIRIO [*shouts*]: Mother! Mother!

ADELA: Let me go!

[BERNARDA *enters. She wears petticoats and a black shawl.*]

BERNARDA: Quiet! Quiet! How poor I am without even a man to help me!

MARTIRIO [*pointing to* ADELA]: She was with him. Look at those skirts covered with straw!

BERNARDA [*going furiously toward* ADELA]: That's the bed of a bad woman!

ADELA [*facing her*]: There'll be an end to prison voices here!

[ADELA *snatches away her mother's cane and breaks it in two.*]

This is what I do with the tyrant's cane. Not another step. No one but Pepe commands me!

[MAGDALENA *enters.*]

MAGDALENA: Adela!

[PONCIA *and* ANGUSTIAS *enter.*]

ADELA: I'm his.

[*To* ANGUSTIAS]

Know that – and go out in the yard and tell him. He'll be master in this house.

ANGUSTIAS: My God!

BERNARDA: The gun! Where's the gun?

[*She rushes out.* PONCIA *runs ahead of her.* AMELIA *enters and looks on frightened, leaning her head against the wall. Behind her comes* MARTIRIO.]

ADELA: No one can hold me back!

[*She tries to go out.*]

ANGUSTIAS [*holding her*]: You're not getting out of here with your body's triumph! Thief! Disgrace of this house!

MAGDALENA: Let her go where we'll never see her again!

[*A shot is heard.*]

BERNARDA [*entering*]: Just try looking for him now!

MARTIRIO [*entering*]: That does away with Pepe el Romano.

ADELA: Pepe! My God! Pepe!

[*She runs out.*]

PONCIA: Did you kill him?

MARTIRIO: No. He raced away on his mare!

BERNARDA: It was my fault. A woman can't aim.

MAGDALENA: Then, why did you say . . . ?

MARTIRIO: For her! I'd like to pour a river of blood over her head!

PONCIA: Curse you!

MAGDALENA: Devil!

BERNARDA: Although it's better this way!

[*A thud is heard.*]

Adela! Adela!

PONCIA [*at her door*]: Open this door!

BERNARDA: Open! Don't think the walls will hide your shame!

SERVANT [*entering*]: All the neighbours are up!

BERNARDA [*in a low voice, but like a roar*]: Open! Or I'll knock the door down!

[*Pause. Everything is silent.*]

Adela!

[*She walks away from the door.*]

A hammer!

[PONCIA *throws herself against the door. It opens and she goes in.
As she enters, she screams and backs out.*]

What is it?

PONCIA [*she puts her hands to her throat*]: May we never die like that!

[*The* SISTERS *fall back. The* SERVANT *crosses herself.* BERNARDA
screams and goes forward.]

Don't go in!

BERNARDA: No, not I! Pepe, you're running now, alive, in the darkness, under the trees, but another day you'll fall. Cut her down!
My daughter died a virgin. Take her to another room and dress
her as though she were a virgin. No one will say anything about
this! She died a virgin. Tell them, so that at dawn, the bells will
ring twice.

MARTIRIO: A thousand times happy she who had him.

BERNARDA: And I want no weeping. Death must be looked at face
to face. Silence!

[*To one daughter*]

Be still, I said!

[*To another daughter*]

Tears when you're alone! We'll drown ourselves in a sea of
mourning. She, the youngest daughter of Bernarda Alba, died a
virgin. Did you hear me? Silence, silence, I said. Silence!

CURTAIN

CHRONOLOGY

of the life of Federico García Lorca

1898. 5 June. Federico García Lorca born at Fuente-vaqueros, near Granada.

1915. First poems written down.

1918. Published his first book, *Impresiones y Paisajes* (prose).

1920. Production of his first play, *El Maleficio de la Mariposa* (verse) in Madrid.

1921. *Libro de Poemas.*

1923. Law degree, University of Granada.

1927. *Mariana Pineda* produced with success in Madrid; García Lorca's drawings attract attention in Barcelona gallery.

1928. *Romancero Gitano.*

1929–30. In the United States and Cuba.

1930. On his return, *The Shoemaker's Prodigious Wife* a success in Madrid.

1931. *Cante Jondo.*

1933. Director of the travelling university-theatre, La Barraca; *Blood Wedding* and *Don Perlimplín* performed in Madrid; to Argentina to lecture; directed his own plays and the classics in Buenos Aires.

1934. *Yerma* produced in Madrid.

1935. The puppet play, *Retablillo de Don Cristóbel*, produced in Madrid; *Llanta por Ignacio Sánchez Mejías* published; *Bitter Oleander (Blood Wedding)* performed in New York; *Doña Rosita* first performed in Barcelona.

1936. July. During the time when the Falangists were occupying Granada, Federico García Lorca was killed and his body thrown into an unmarked grave.

MORE ABOUT PENGUINS

Penguinews, which appears every month, contains details of all the new books issued by Penguins as they are published. From time to time it is supplemented by *Penguins in Print*, which is a complete list of all books published by Penguins which are in print. (There are well over three thousand of these.)

A specimen copy of *Penguinews* will be sent to you free on request, and you can become a subscriber for the price of the postage – 4s. for a year's issues (including the complete lists). Just write to Dept EP, Penguin Books Ltd, Harmondsworth, Middlesex, enclosing a cheque or postal order, and your name will be added to the mailing list.

Two other books published by Penguins are described on the following pages.

Note: *Penguinews* and *Penguins in Print*
are not available in the U.S.A. or Canada

New American Drama

THE AMERICAN DREAM: EDWARD ALBEE
GALLOWS HUMOUR: JACK RICHARDSON
THE TYPISTS: MURRAY SCHISGAL
INCIDENT AT VICHY: ARTHUR MILLER

EDITED BY CHARLES MAROWITZ

The four plays in this volume represent in their different ways the best of the new theatre of America. Edward Albee, author of *Who's Afraid of Virginia Woolf?*, has already made a considerable impact as one of the most exciting dramatists to appear in recent years. Murray Schisgal has won admiration from critics on both sides of the Atlantic, and Jack Richardson is beginning to be recognized as an important and highly original theatrical talent. Even Arthur Miller, established figure though he is, has made, in *Incident at Vichy*, a new and thoughtful departure that represents an important addition to his works.

NOT FOR SALE IN THE U.S.A.